THE BEST
ADVICE EVER

FOR

LEADERS

Other Books by Wess Roberts

Leadership Secrets of Attila the Hun
Straight A's Never Made Anybody Rich
Victory Secrets of Attila the Hun
Make It So (with Bill Ross)
Protect Your Achilles Heel
It Takes More Than a Carrot and a Stick

THE BEST
ADVICE EVER

FOR

LEADERS

COMPILED AND EDITED BY
WESS ROBERTS, PH.D.

**Andrews McMeel
Publishing**

Kansas City

02 03 04 05 06 RDH 10 9 8 7 6 5 4 3 2 1

Library of Congress Cataloging-in-Publication Data
The best advice ever for leaders / compiled and edited by Wess Roberts, Ph.D.
     p. cm.
  ISBN 0-7407-2202-6
    1. Leadership—Quotations, maxims, etc. I. Roberts, Wess.
HD57.7 .B475 2002
658.4'092—dc21   2001053445

For all who desire to lead,
for all who desire to improve their leadership,
and for all who desire to think about
how well they are doing as leaders.

ACKNOWLEDGMENTS

Many thanks to Justin and Christine, Jaime and Jared, Jeremy, and Cheryl for their assistance. Many thanks to Allan Stark for suggesting this project to me. Many thanks to my editor, Patrick Dobson, and the staff of Andrews McMeel Publishing, who made this project a success.

INTRODUCTION

The ability to inspire, give direction, and pull people together is crucial in every organization and in all human endeavors. Although there are few absolute, hard-and-fast rules for successful leadership, there are some leadership principles and ideas that have universal application for people in any country or period of time. Because many aspects of human behavior are universal, good advice for leading others can transcend cultural, geographical, and historical boundaries, so that leaders can benefit from such advice whoever they are or wherever they may be.

The Best Advice Ever for Leaders takes this approach by collecting ideas from a vast range of leaders from virtually every walk of life, every part of the world, and every era of human history. By examining such an array of ideas, we find that valuable and time-tested advice for leaders comes from such diverse figures as George Washington and Lao-tzu, Julius Caesar and Oprah Winfrey, Lee Iacocca and Mark Twain, and many, many others. By studying such a wide range of thoughts and perspectives, a leader's own perspective broadens greatly, and he or she is much better able to help people in innumerable situations attain their goals.

However, although valid and insightful leadership advice is as good in twenty-first-century America as it was in ancient China or Europe in the Renaissance, understanding who the person is and something about his or her life will greatly improve our ability to put his or her thoughts and advice in context, and hopefully to get more meaning from the idea than the words alone. For this reason, *The Best Advice Ever for Leaders* also contains notes about the backgrounds and accomplishments of the figures whose ideas are found in the following pages. It is organized in a series of running topics, each of which imparts an important piece of insight or wisdom pertaining to the characteristics of good leadership and how to build, use, and maintain them.

Of course, not every bit of wisdom in this book will be applicable to every circumstance or meaningful to every person at the same time or in the same way. Yet this only emphasizes the importance of studying leadership with an open mind and a desire for diversity so that we may take whatever advice is helpful and useful for us as our situations dictate. In fact, the greatest leaders throughout history have sought wisdom from as many sources as possible in order to have a complete picture of how to lead to win, how to adapt to changing events, and how to relate better to the multitude of different personalities among the people they lead.

In the end, I hope the title of this book speaks for itself. I hope you will benefit and improve on your ability to lead others when you thoughtfully consider the ideas and experiences of other leaders. And, most important, I hope you will find principles in this book that you will use in helping others succeed, because it is putting it to use that will truly make this *The Best Advice Ever for Leaders*.

—ACCOUNTABILITY—

The ultimate result of shielding men from the effects of folly is to fill the world with fools.

*—Herbert Spencer, 1820–1903, English philosopher
and sociologist who originated social Darwinism
and coined the phrase "survival of the fittest"*

That's the penalty we have to pay for our acts of foolishness—someone else always suffers for them.

*—Alfred Sutro, 1863–1933, British dramatist who translated the
works of Maurice Maeterlinck and was a popular playwright himself*

Victory has a hundred fathers, but defeat is an orphan.

*—Galeazzo Ciano (Conte di Cortellazzo), 1903–1944, minister of
foreign affairs and secretary of state for press and propaganda in
Mussolini's Italy. Ciano married Mussolini's daughter, Edda.
Notwithstanding, Ciano helped force the Italian dictator's
resignation, which led to Ciano's assassination by Mussolini's allies.*

—ACHIEVEMENT—

Not everything that is more difficult is more meritorious.

*—Thomas Aquinas, 1225–1274, Italian Dominican friar
and noted Scholastic philosopher who introduced
Aristotle's work to Christian Western Europe*

Be studious in your profession, and you will be learned. Be industrious and frugal, and you will be rich. Be sober and temperate, and you will be healthy. Be in general virtuous, and you will be happy. At least you will, by such conduct, stand the best chances for such consequence.

—Benjamin Franklin, 1706–1790. As statesman, writer, and scientist, Franklin was active in framing the Declaration of Independence and laid the foundation for public libraries.

We throw all our attention on the utterly idle question whether A has done as well as B, when the only question is whether A has done as well as he could.

—William Graham Sumner, 1840–1910, American economist, sociologist, and Yale University professor. Sumner was a proponent of social Darwinism, sound currency, and free trade, and he opposed socialism.

Mastery is not something that strikes in an instant, like a thunderbolt, but a gathering power that moves steadily through time, like weather.

—John Champlin Gardner Jr., 1933–1982, American author, educator, and lecturer who wrote fiction, children's books, poetry, radio plays, and scholarly medieval studies and believed in a higher moral purpose in writing fiction

—ADVERSITY—

If all our misfortunes were laid in one common heap whence everyone must take an equal portion, most people would be contented to take their own and depart.

—Socrates, c. 470–399 B.C., Greek philosopher

Adversity is the trial principle. Without it a man hardly knows whether he is honest or not.

*—Henry Fielding, 1707–1754, English novelist who provoked
the introduction of censorship in theaters with his
political satire* The Historical Register for 1736

It is not true that suffering ennobles the character; happiness does that sometimes, but suffering, for the most part, makes men petty and vindictive.

*—William Somerset Maugham, 1874–1965, English novelist
and playwright who wrote* Of Human Bondage

We could never learn to be brave and patient if there were only joy in the world.

*—Helen Keller, 1880–1968, American writer, academic, and social
reformer who, despite being deaf and blind from the age of
nineteen months, learned to speak, read Braille, and type*

If you have a job without aggravations, you don't have a job.

> —*Malcolm Forbes, 1919–1990, American publisher,* Forbes *magazine. Forbes used his magazine and books to praise the virtues of laissez-faire capitalism. He was the first person to fly coast to coast across the United States in a hot air balloon and was an avid motorcycle enthusiast.*

—ADVICE—

Never trust the advice of a man in difficulties.

> —*Aesop, fl. sixth century B.C., Greek storyteller thought to have been a slave and adviser to King Croesus of Lydia. He is the reputed author of* Aesop's Fables.

Commanders should be counseled, chiefly, by persons of known talent, by those who have made an art of war their particular study, and whose knowledge is derived from experience; from those who are present at the scene of action, who see the country, who see the enemy, who see the advantages that occasions offer, and who, like people embarked in the same ship, are sharers of the danger.

> —*Lucius Aemilius Paulus, fl. 229–160 B.C., Roman general, praetor in Spain, and consul*

The true secret of giving advice is, after you have honestly given it, to be perfectly indifferent whether it is taken or not and never persist in trying to set people right.

> —*Hannah Whitall Smith, 1832–1911, American religious leader and founder of the Woman's Christian Temperance Union*

We should be careful and discriminating in all the advice we give; we should be especially careful in giving advice that we would not think of following ourselves. Most of all, we ought to avoid giving counsel which we don't follow when it damages those who take us at our word.

—Adlai E. Stevenson, 1900–1965, American Democratic politician, governor of Illinois, and U.S. delegate to the United Nations. Stevenson also served in the Department of the Navy and the State Department. He was a candidate for the presidency in 1952 and 1956. Eloquence and wit characterized Stevenson's speeches. He is the author of Friends and Enemies.

We must all consult doctors, lawyers, bankers, and other specialists to help us, but view experts with a jaundiced eye. Trust your own knowledge and instincts. When something sounds fishy, ask, "Says who? Where is it written?" Is the expert there to help you—or to attend to a bigger client, to please the boss, to get personal visibility or to win a better job? Never assume that so-called professionalism will protect you.

—David Mahoney, 1923–2000, president, Good Humor Company; president and COO, Norton Simon; and CEO, the Charles A. Dana Foundation. Mahoney was the first American executive to be paid a million-dollar salary. After leaving the corporate world, Mahoney became heavily involved in funding and raising funds for brain research.

When you lie down with dogs, you can't be shocked to get fleas. When you lie down with a wolf, you must count yourself lucky to come out with your jugular intact.

> —*Sarah Ferguson, b. 1959, British author, corporate spokesperson, and the Duchess of York, from* My Story. *After divorcing Prince Andrew, Ferguson became a spokesperson for Weight Watchers. She is the author of a series of children's books about Budgie the Little Helicopter and is the founder of Children in Crisis.*

—ANGER MANAGEMENT—

Anybody can become angry—that is easy; but to be angry with the right person, and to the right degree, and at the right time, and for the right purpose, and in the right way— that is not within everybody's power and is not easy.

—Aristotle, 384–322 B.C., Greek philosopher, scientist, and physician

—APOLOGY—

It is a good rule in life never to apologize. The right sort of people do not want apologies, and the wrong sort take mean advantage of them.

—P. G. Wodehouse, 1881–1975, English novelist, author of
The Inimitable Jeeves, *and collaborator with Guy Bolton in writing the musical comedy* The Cabaret Girl. *He was a prisoner of war in Germany during World War II. Wodehouse became a U.S. citizen in 1955.*

—APPEASERS—

Appeasers believe that if you keep throwing steaks to a tiger, the tiger will become a vegetarian.

—Heywood Broun, 1888–1939, American journalist, columnist, and author. Broun was on the staff of the New York Morning Telegraph, Tribune, World, World-Telegram, *and* Post. *He wrote a column, "It Seems to Me."*

—ARGUMENTS—

Fools must be rejected not by arguments, but by facts.

> —*Flavius Josephus, c. 37–105, Judaean general, historian, and politician, and governor of Galilee. Josephus spent three years in the desert living as a hermit before joining the Pharisee sect. He was a leader in the failed Jewish revolt against the Romans.*

Never contend with a man who has nothing to lose.

> —*Baltasar Gracián y Morales, 1601–1658, Spanish Jesuit writer and author of* El criticón, *the philosophical novel examining civilization by way of its effects on a savage*

Arguments out of a petty mouth are unanswerable.

> —*Joseph Addison, 1672–1719, British Whig politician, essayist, poet, and dramatist. Among other positions held, Addison was a member of Parliament and secretary of state. He also co-founded the* Spectator *and is considered one of the masters of English prose.*

I never make the mistake of arguing with people for whose opinion I have no respect.

> —*Edward Gibbon, 1737–1794, English historian best known for his book* The Decline and Fall of the Roman Empire

Quarrel not at all. No man resolved to make the most of himself can spare time for personal contention. Still less can he afford to take all the consequences, including the vitiating of his temper and loss of self-control. Yield larger things to which you can show no more equal right; and yield lesser ones, though clearly your own. Better give your path to a dog than be bitten by him in contesting for the right. Even killing the dog would not cure the bite.

> —*Abraham Lincoln, 1809–1865, sixteenth president of the United States. Lincoln worked as a surveyor, postmaster, and lawyer. As president, he wrote the Emancipation Proclamation. His most noted speech, "The Gettysburg Address," is also one of the most admired speeches in world history.*

Most quarrels amplify a misunderstanding.

> —*André Gide, 1869–1951, French writer whose works include stories, satires, and fables. He was awarded a Nobel Prize in 1947.*

The most savage controversies are those about matters as to which there is no good evidence either way.

> —*Bertrand Russell, 1872–1970, English philosopher, mathematician, author, social reformer, and conscientious objector during World War I. He later campaigned against nuclear arms and for women's rights and was awarded a Nobel Prize in 1950.*

What convinces is conviction. Believe in the argument you're advancing. If you don't, you're as good as dead. The other person will sense something isn't there, and no chain of reasoning, no matter how logical or elegant or brilliant, will win your case for you.

> —*Lyndon B. Johnson, 1908–1973, thirty-sixth president of the United States*

—ARROGANCE—

Hector, there is no persuading you to take advice. Because heaven has so richly endowed you with the arts of war, you think that you must therefore excel others in counsel; but you cannot thus claim preeminence in all things. Heaven has made one man an excellent soldier; of another it has made a dancer or a singer and player on the lyre; while yet in another Jove has implanted a wise understanding of which men reap fruit to the saving of many . . .

—Polydamas to Hector before Troy, from Homer's Iliad,
as translated by Samuel Butler

—AUTHORITY—

Little is done where many command.

—Dutch proverb

Authority without wisdom is like a heavy ax without an edge, fitter to bruise than to polish.

—Anne Bradstreet, 1612–1672, English-born American poet

Since no man has a natural authority over his fellow, and force creates no right, we must conclude that conventions form the basis of all legitimate authority among men.

*—Jean-Jacques Rousseau, 1712–1778, Swiss-born
French philosopher and writer whose acclaimed essay
"Discours sur les arts et sciences" presents the notion
that the savage state is superior to the civilized*

Mere precedent is a dangerous source of authority.

>—*Andrew Jackson, 1767–1845, seventh president of the United States. Jackson was also a lawyer, Tennessee Supreme Court judge, governor of the Florida Territory, and army major general.*

The majority of men . . . are not capable of thinking, but only of believing, and . . . are not accessible to reason, but only to authority.

>—*Arthur Schopenhauer, 1788–1860, German philosopher who expounded pessimism and the irrational impulses of life arising from the will*

Authority forgets a dying king.

>—*Alfred Tennyson, 1809–1892, English poet, poet laureate of England, and author of* The Charge of the Light Brigade

—BRAVERY—

If we take the generally accepted definition of bravery as a quality which knows no fear, I have never seen a brave man. All men are frightened. The more intelligent they are, the more frightened.

>—*George S. Patton Jr., 1885–1945, American army general whose 2nd Armored Division received its "Hell on Wheels" motto while under his command at Fort Benning, Georgia*

—BUSINESS—

No business which depends for existence on paying less than living wages to its workers has any right to continue in this country. By business I mean the whole of commerce as well as the whole of industry; by workers I mean all workers— the white-collar class as well as the bare subsistence level— by living wages, I mean the wages of decent living.

—Franklin D. Roosevelt, 1882–1945, thirty-second president of the United States, the only president elected to four terms. He is most noted for his New Deal programs, which included the Social Security Act, the Fair Labor Standards Act, and the Federal Housing Administration.

Watch out for the fourth "E." There are five "E's" in business. They are Excitement, Enthusiasm, Exuberance, Euphoria, and Extinction. The five E's happen in order. At first, you get Excited about the things you are doing in your company and with the products or technologies. You next become Enthusiastic because things are moving along successfully, which is followed by Exuberance and a more intense feeling of satisfaction and accomplishment. But once you reach Euphoria, where you feel as if nothing can go wrong, step five, Extinction, surely and automatically ensues.

—Ray Noorda, b. 1924, founder and CEO, Novell Inc.

—CHANGE—

Change is not made without inconvenience, even from worse to better.

> —*Richard Hooker, 1554–1600, English theologian and staunch Anglican. His book* Of the Laws of Ecclesiastical Polity *established the Anglican position versus the Roman Catholic and Puritan.*

When it is not necessary to change, it is necessary not to change.

> —*Lucius Cary, c. 1610–1643, British royal and author*

The search for a new personality is futile; what is fruitful is the human interest the old personality can take in new activities.

> —*Cesare Pavese, 1908–1950, Italian writer, publisher, and translator who founded the publishing house Einaudi and was imprisoned for his anti-fascist activities. Much of his writing centered on alienation and disillusionment in modern life.*

Sometimes if you want to see a change for the better, you have to take things into your own hands.

> —*Clint Eastwood, b. 1930, actor and director. Eastwood gained fame with* A Fistful of Dollars, *the first cult "spaghetti western" film shot in Italy. He has also been mayor of Carmel, California.*

—CHARACTER—

It is not the oath that makes us believe the man, but the man the oath.

—Aeschylus, 525–456 B.C., Greek tragic dramatist, soldier, and author of Agamemnon. *Aeschylus served in the Athenian army in the Persian wars and created true drama of action.*

Our character is not so much the product of race and heredity, as of circumstances by which nature forms habits, by which we are nourished and live.

—Marcus Tullius Cicero, 106–43 B.C., Roman orator, lawyer, statesman, soldier, and philosopher who supported Pompey against Julius Caesar but reconciled with Caesar after the battle of Pharsalus

No one ever became extremely wicked suddenly.

—Juvenal, c. 60–127, Roman rhetorician and satirical poet. Juvenal was brutally frank in his attacks on the vices of Rome under the empire.

I hate the man who is double-minded, kind in words but a foe in his conduct.

—Palladius of Helenopolis, c. 365–425, Galatian Christian ecclesiastic, historian, and bishop of Bithynia

Character is much easier kept than recovered.

—Thomas Paine, 1737–1809, English-born American revolutionary, pamphleteer, political philosopher, and author of Common Sense *and* The Age of Reason. *In late life, he lost his standing, was ostracized, and lived in poverty.*

The greatest man is he who chooses the right with invincible resolution, who resists the sorest temptations from within and without, who bears the heaviest burdens cheerfully, who is calmest in storms and most fearless under menace and frowns, whose reliance on truth, on virtue, on God, is most unfaltering.

—*William Ellery Channing, 1780–1842, American transcendentalist colleague of Thoreau and Emerson. Channing was a liberal congregationalist who became known as "the apostle of Unitarianism." He is the author of* Negro Slavery *and* Self Culture.

The measure of a man's real character is what he would do if he knew he would never be found out.

—*Thomas Babington Macaulay, 1800–1859, English noble, politician, historian, and author of* History of England

Every man has three characters: that which he shows, that which he has, and that which he thinks he has.

—*Alphonse Karr, 1808–1890, French journalist and novelist who was editor of* Figaro *and founder of the satirical review* Les Guêpes

As I grow older, I pay less attention to what men say. I just watch what they do.

—*Andrew Carnegie, 1835–1919, Scottish-born CEO, U.S. Steel Corporation. After his retirement, Carnegie devoted himself to distributing his huge fortune to benefit society, founded Carnegie Institute of Technology, and helped finance public libraries in numerous small towns throughout the United States.*

In each human heart are a tiger, a pig, an ass, and a nightingale. Diversity of character is due to their unequal activity.

—*Ambrose Bierce, c. 1842–1914, American journalist and author. Bierce served in the Union army during the Civil War. He became known as a witty and caustic writer and contributed a column of "Prattle" in the* San Francisco Examiner. *One of his most popular works was* The Devil's Dictionary. *He mysteriously disappeared in Mexico in 1914.*

Duty—Honor—Country. Those three hallowed words reverently dictate what you ought to be, what you can be, what you will be. They are your rallying points; to build courage when courage seems to fail; to regain faith when there seems to be little cause for faith; to create hope when hope becomes forlorn. . . . They build your basic character; they mold you for your future roles. . . . They make you strong enough to know when you are weak, and brave enough to face yourself when you are afraid. They teach you to be proud and unbending in honest failure, but humble and gentle in success, not to substitute words for actions, not to seek the path of comfort, but to face the stress and spur of difficulty and challenge; to learn to stand up in the storm but to have compassion on those who fail; to master yourself before you seek to master others; to have a heart that is clean, a goal that is high; to learn to laugh yet never forget how to weep; to reach into the future yet never neglect the past; to be serious yet never to take yourself too seriously; to be modest so that you will remember the simplicity of true greatness, the open mind of true wisdom, the meekness of true strength. They give you a temper of the will, a quality of the imagination, a vigor of the emotions, a freshness of the deep springs of life, a temperamental predominance of courage over timidity, an appetite for adventure over love of ease. They create in your heart the sense of wonder, the unfailing hope of what next, and the joy and inspiration of life.

> —*Douglas MacArthur, 1880–1964, from his address to the Corps of Cadets at the United States Military Academy, May 12, 1962. MacArthur was the supreme Allied commander in the Southwest Pacific during World War II and of the occupation forces in Japan. He accepted the Japanese surrender aboard the U.S.S.* Missouri *on September 2, 1945. Despite being dismissed by President Truman as supreme commander of U.N. Forces in Korea for publicly advocating an invasion of China, MacArthur has been called an "American Caesar" and perhaps the greatest battlefield commander in American history.*

Character isn't inherited. One builds it daily by the way one thinks and acts, thought by thought, action by action. If one lets fear or hate or anger take possession of the mind, they become self-forged chains.

—Helen Gahagan Douglas, 1900–1980, American actor and politician who became a Broadway star at the age of twenty-two. After moving to California, Douglas became interested in politics over the misery of displaced "Okies." Douglas was elected to the U.S. House of Representatives in 1944, where she was a thoughtful and consistent New Deal Democrat who worked tirelessly for liberal programs. In 1950, Douglas ran for the Senate but was soundly defeated by Richard Nixon, who waged an inspiring red-baiting campaign against her. Douglas never again ran for public office but remained a public speaker and activist until her death.

Conversely, just as non-conformity in behavior does not necessarily mean non-conformity in character, so utter conformity in behavior may be purchased by the individual at so high a price as to lead to a character neurosis.

> —*David Riesman, b. 1909, American sociologist, lawyer, writer, and professor at the University of Chicago and Harvard University. He is the author of* The Lonely Crowd.

No one wants to follow a weak leader. He is the worst kind. You cannot rely on his judgment because you don't know what he will do in a difficult situation. Much more respect and loyalty are given to the tough leader, the one who is not afraid to make difficult and even unpopular decisions, just as long as he is perceived to be decent and fair and reliable in his dealings with his subordinates.

> —*Harold Geneen, 1910–1997, CEO, International Telephone and Telegraph (ITT). Geneen transformed a stodgy ITT into 150 affiliated companies operating in fifty-seven countries.*

Your character, as a source of managerial influence, is the degree to which others respect your personal commitment not to allow them to wind up with the short end of the stick if they take you at your word. If they do not see such a personal commitment as characteristic of you, then to that extent your influence will be weakened.

> —*William Oncken Jr., 1912–1988, American writer, lecturer, and management trainer, from* Managing Management Time. *Oncken worked on the Manhattan Project and at the Naval Ordnance Laboratory during World War II. He later applied his training and experience as a physicist to arrive at an understanding of human behavior in organizations.*

If you don't have a foundation of life, a moral foundation, all else is ephemeral.

—Steve Forbes, b. 1947, American journalist, lecturer, and president and CEO of Forbes Inc., in The New Republic, *April 27, 1998. Forbes used his own money to conduct his surprisingly strong, but ultimately unsuccessful, campaign to become the Republican candidate for president of the United States in 1996. He is widely admired throughout the world for his vision and ideas for shaping the future of both individual opportunity and economic security.*

—CHARISMA—

Charisma: Some leaders have it, some leaders don't. The very best leaders have it in abundance. Deep down, every leader wants it. With a determined effort any leader can develop some degree of charisma. Like good leadership, charisma starts with an enthusiastic, positive, joyful approach to life in general. This inner strength, when properly cultivated and expressed, strikes a chord in others, enabling a leader to bring out the best in them. True caring about others is the critical element that translates the personality of a leader into the catalyst that results in charismatic leadership. Caring consists of a genuine understanding for the needs and aspirations of others and a demonstrated willingness to act on their behalf. Mere words are not enough. Caring starts by looking others in the eye when you talk to them and listening to them when they talk to you. Charismatic leaders are also outstanding mentors and developers of their subordinates. This ability springs from a corresponding desire to have successful, highly motivated people working for you.

—John C. "Doc" Bahnsen, b. 1934, American army brigadier general who was awarded eighteen medals for gallantry in Vietnam and was greatly admired by the soldiers he commanded

—CHOICE—

Not choice, but habit, rules the unreflecting herd.

> —*William Wordsworth, 1770–1850, English poet and poet
> laureate of England whose* Lyrical Ballads, *composed with
> Samuel Taylor Coleridge, includes "Tintern Abbey,"
> regarded as a landmark in romanticism*

You always do what you want to do. This is true with every act. You may say you had to do something, or that you were forced to, but actually, whatever you choose to do, you do by choice. Only you have the power to choose for yourself.

> —*W. Clement Stone, b. 1902, president and founder of
> Combined Insurance Company of America and Success
> Unlimited. Known as "Mr. PMA" (positive mental attitude),
> Stone co-authored, with Napoleon Hill,* Success Through
> a Positive Mental Attitude. *His typical greeting is said
> to be "I feel great; I feel wonderful. How are you?"*

Everything can be taken from a man but one thing: the last of the human freedoms—to choose one's attitude in any given set of circumstances, to choose one's own way.

> —*Viktor E. Frankl, 1905–1997, Austrian and American psychologist
> and educator. Frankl was held in four concentration camps during
> World War II, including Auschwitz and Dachau, where he tried to
> help other inmates suffering from severe depression. Frankl's
> parents, brother, and pregnant wife were all killed in concentration
> camps. He went on to create a therapeutic process known as
> logotherapy, which encourages patients to find meaning in
> their lives, and spent the later years of his career lecturing
> at several universities in the United States.*

—CIRCUMSTANCES—

Men are dependent on circumstances, not circumstances on men.

> —*Herodotus, 484–425 B.C., Greek historian considered*
> *"the father of history" because he was the first*
> *historian to approach his craft scientifically*

—CLEAR THINKING—

All men who deliberate on controversial matters should be free from hate, friendship, anger, and pity.

> —*Sallust, 86–34 B.C., Roman historian, politician, and author of*
> History of the Roman Republic. *He was born Gaius Sallustius*
> *Crispus and was a partisan of Julius Caesar. He was expelled*
> *from the senate for alleged immorality. He amassed a huge*
> *personal fortune while governor of Numidia.*

Freethinkers are those who are willing to use their minds without prejudice and without fearing to understand things that clash with their own customs, privileges, or beliefs. This state of mind is not common, but it is essential for right thinking; where it is absent, discussion is apt to become worse than useless.

> —*Lev Nikolayevich Tolstoy, 1828–1910, Russian count, moral*
> *philosopher, soldier, and writer. After a spiritual transformation, he*
> *developed a form of Christian anarchism and devoted himself to*
> *social reform. He is the author of* War and Peace *and* Anna Karenina.

—COACHING—

Start by teaching the fundamentals, A player's got to know the basics of the game and how to play his position. Next, keep him in line. That's discipline. The men have to play as a team, not a bunch of individuals. . . . Then you've got to care for one another. You've got to love one another. . . . Most people call it team spirit.

> —*Vince Lombardi, 1913–1970, coach of the Green Bay Packers who took the team to five National Football League championships and two Super Bowl titles*

Some guys, in order to get their attention, you have to holler at them and fine them. There are other guys you can't. Some guys you holler at them, they crawl into a shell. Some guys you holler at them, they lose their confidence. You gotta always try to do everything you can to help them maintain that confidence level.

> —*Tommy Lasorda, b. 1927, American baseball player and manager of the Los Angeles Dodgers*

—COMMITMENT—

What keeps so many employees back is simply unwillingness to pay the price, to make the exertion, the effort to sacrifice their ease and comfort.

> —*Orison Swett Marden, 1850–1924, founder of* Success Magazine *and considered to be the founder of the success movement in America*

Nothing in the world can take the place of persistence. Talent will not; nothing is more common than unsuccessful men with talent. Genius will not; unrewarded genius is almost a proverb. Education will not; the world is full of educated derelicts. Persistence and determination alone are omnipotent.

—Calvin Coolidge, 1872–1933, thirtieth president of the United States, who had no vice president during his first term in office

Don't rush to follow through on an idea until you, by yourself, find yourself getting excited about it. If you are going to become a champion of a new idea, a new method, or a new product, make sure you're a believer before you become a preacher.

—Harold J. Leavitt, b. 1922, professor at Stanford and Carnegie-Mellon universities and author of Corporate Pathfinders

Ambiguous commitment produces mediocre results.

—Harvey Mackay, b. 1933, CEO of Mackay Envelope Corporation, civic leader, and author of Sharkproof

—COMMON SENSE—

Common sense is judgment without reflection which is shared by an entire class, a people, a nation, or the whole human race.

—Giambattista Vico, 1668–1744, Italian jurist, educator, and philosopher known for his effort to discover and organize laws common to the evolution of all society

—COMMUNICATION—

Words differently arranged have a different meaning, and meanings differently arranged have a different effect.

—Blaise Pascal, 1623–1662, French mathematician, physicist, and religious philosopher best known for deriving the principle that the pressure of a fluid at rest is transmitted equally in all directions. He also created probability theory and was a believer in Jansenistic Christianity, a system of religious doctrine based on moral determinism.

Remember, gentlemen, an order that can be misunderstood will be misunderstood.

> —*Helmuth Karl Bernhard Moltke, 1800–1891, Prussian count and army field marshal who devised strategic and tactical command methods for modern mass armies engaged on broad fronts*

People think that I can teach them style. What stuff all is! Have something to say, and say it as clearly as you can. This is the only secret to style.

> —*Matthew Arnold, 1822–1888, English critic, poet, and professor at Oxford*

Words can destroy. What we call each other ultimately becomes what we think of each other, and it matters.

> —*Jeane J. Kirkpatrick, b. 1926, American political scientist and U.S. representative to the United Nations*

—COMPASSION—

We live very close together. So, our prime purpose in life is to help others. And if you can't help them, at least don't hurt them.

> —*Dalai Lama, b. 1935, spiritual and temporal head of Tibet, born Tenzin Gyatso, who was forced into exile in India by Chinese suppression in 1959. He was awarded a Nobel Prize in 1989.*

—COMPETENCE—

A competent leader can get efficient service from poor troops, while on the contrary an incapable leader can demoralize the best of troops.

> —*John J. "Black Jack" Pershing, 1860–1948, American army general who commanded the American Expeditionary Force in World War I and was awarded a Pulitzer Prize in 1931*

—COMPETITION—

Of all powers operating on the affairs of mankind, none is greater than that of competition.

> —*Henry Clay, 1777–1852, American orator and U.S. secretary of state whose attempts to hold the United States together in face of the slavery issue earned him the nickname of "the Great Pacificator." He also earned the nickname "the Great Compromiser" for his oratory favoring the Compromise of 1850.*

There is no kind of ultimate goal to do something twice as good as anyone else can. It's just to do the job as best you can. If it turns out good, fine. If it doesn't, that's the way it goes.

> —*Charles E. "Chuck" Yeager, b. 1923, American air force brigadier general. On October 14, 1947, flying the rocket-powered X-1 fighter plane, Yeager became the first person to pilot an aircraft faster than the speed of sound.*

Scene stealing is as endemic to movie sets as cameras and lights, but theft requires two people: one to steal, one to give it away. Actors and actresses who without a struggle permit another to unfairly diminish a performance deserve what usually happens—professional oblivion. Performers in a cast are not friendly souls adrift in a comfortable cockleshell. Even when benign winds and following wavelets propel their craft to mutual success, they remain individual competitors in a common cause.

> —*Shirley Temple Black, b. 1928, American actor, diplomat, and corporate board member, from* Child Star. *Temple, who starred in more than forty films, began acting at the age of three and was the number-one box office attraction from 1935–1938. She later served as U.S. representative to the United Nations and U.S. ambassador to the Republic of Ghana.*

Competition is easier to accept if you realize it is not an act of aggression or abrasion. . . . I've worked with my best friends in direct competition. Whatever you want in life, other people are going to want too. Believe in yourself enough to accept the idea that you have an equal right to it.

> —*Diane Sawyer, b. 1945, American television journalist and co-host of* Good Morning America, PrimeTime Live, *and* Turning Point. *Sawyer went to Washington to help President Nixon write his memoirs and earned a reputation for integrity with the news industry. She was the first woman to be a correspondent for* 60 Minutes.

—COMPROMISE—

A compromise is the art of dividing a cake in such a way that everyone believes that he has got the biggest piece.

> —*Ludwig Erhard, 1897–1977, German economist and chancellor of West Germany. Erhard also served as the director of the Economic Council for the Anglo-U.S. Occupation Zone and as federal economics minister.*

It is never right to compromise with dishonesty.

> —*Henry Cabot Lodge Jr., 1902–1985, U.S. representative to the United Nations, ambassador to South Vietnam, and chief U.S. negotiator at the Vietnam peace talks in Paris*

Compromise does not mean cowardice.

> —*John F. Kennedy, 1917–1963, thirty-fifth president of the United States. He served as a naval officer in World War II and was a member of the House and Senate before becoming the first Roman Catholic elected president. Kennedy won a Pulitzer Prize in 1957 for his book,* Profiles in Courage. *His assassination cut short what many believe would have been a presidency of great accomplishments.*

—CONSENSUS—

When two men in business always agree, one of them is unnecessary.

> —*William Wrigley Jr., 1861–1932, founder, William Wrigley Jr. and Company. Wrigley's first business experience with chewing gum was giving it away as an incentive when he worked as a salesman. He invested some of his chewing-gum fortune in hotels and in the Chicago Cubs baseball team.*

—CONTROVERSY—

When a thing ceases to be a subject of controversy, it ceases to be a subject of interest.

> —*William Hazlitt, 1778–1830, English essayist and author. Hazlitt wrote for the* Examiner, Edinburgh Review, London Magazine, *and* Colburn's New Monthly. *He was a drama critic for the* Morning Chronicle. *He also lectured widely on Shakespeare and English drama and is the author of* Life of Napoleon.

—CORPORATIONS—

A corporation is an artificial thing, invisible, intangible, and existing only in the contemplation of the law.

—John Marshall, 1755–1835, chief justice, U.S. Supreme Court.
Marshall served in the Continental Army during the
Revolutionary War. He was a congressman from Virginia
and U.S. secretary of state, and he was the principal founder
of the American system of constitutional law.

—COURAGE—

Fortunately for themselves and the world, nearly all men are cowards and dare not act on what they believe. Nearly all of our disasters come of a few fools having the "courage of their convictions."

—Coventry Patmore, 1823–1896, English poet. Patmore
worked as an assistant librarian in the British Museum.
The themes of his poems were mostly love and religion.

Courage is a special kind of knowledge: the knowledge of how to fear what ought to be feared and how not to fear what ought not to be feared.

—David Ben-Gurion, 1886–1973, Polish-born Israeli politician
who was prime minister, member of Knesset, and chairman
of Zionist Executive. Ben-Gurion was expelled from
Palestine by Turkish authorities for Zionist activities.

If you stand up and be counted, from time to time you may get yourself knocked down. But remember this: A man flattened by an opponent can get up again. A man flattened by conformity stays down for good.

> —*Thomas J. Watson Jr., 1914–1993, CEO, IBM. Watson succeeded his father as chairman of IBM and is considered to be one of the greatest capitalists in history.*

Few men are willing to brave the disapproval of their fellows, the censure of their colleagues, the wrath of their society. Moral courage is a rarer commodity than bravery in battle or great intelligence. Yet it is the one essential, vital quality of those who seek to change a world which yields most painfully to change.

> —*Robert F. Kennedy, 1925–1968, U.S. attorney general and U.S. senator, from his "Day of Affirmation Address," University of Capetown, June 6, 1966. Kennedy served as a seaman second class in the U.S. navy during World War II. Had he not been assassinated while campaigning for the Democratic nomination, it is quite possible that Kennedy would have been elected president of the United States.*

—CREATIVITY—

There is no fixed boundary to human creative potential. You must become unshakably convinced that nothing is impossible. . . . Make your own considered judgments independent of others' "common sense." . . . And in all your endeavors strive to position yourself in the center of the whirlpool.

> —*Kazuo Inamori, b. 1932, Japanese author, lecturer, co-founder of Kyoto Ceramics, president of Kyocera, president of the Inamori Foundation, and founder of Daini Denden, from* The Kyocera Philosophy. *Although he is an ordained Zen Buddhist monk, Inamori eschewed all vows of poverty, silence, and quiescent passivity, and he remains the guiding force behind all aspects of his diverse international businesses.*

—CRITICISM—

Criticism comes easier than craftsmanship.

>—*Zeuxis, fl. 400 B.C., Italian-born Greek painter whose works*
>*are known only through the reports of ancient writers.*
>*Zeuxis is reputed to have painted a picture of a bunch of*
>*grapes with such realism that birds attempted to eat them.*

Never rebuke a man in such a way as to shame him in public.

>—*Rashi, 1040–1105, French Talmudist, poet, and author.*
>*Born Shlomo Yitzhaqi, Rashi gained distinction*
>*by his commentaries on the Old Testament.*

Never giving criticism without praise is a strict rule for me.
No matter what you are criticizing, you must find something good to say—both before and after. . . . Criticize the act, not the person.

>—*Mary Kay Ash, b. 1915, founder and CEO, Mary Kay Inc.*
>*Mary Kay Inc. has over 500,000 independent beauty*
>*consultants in twenty-nine markets worldwide.*

—CRITICS—

A critic is a necessary evil, and criticism is an evil necessity.

> —*Carolyn Wells, 1862–1942, American author of over
> 170 books of humorous sketches, parodies, short stories, novels,
> detective fiction, and juveniles, including* Spooky Hollow

Unless the bastards have the courage to give you unqualified praise, I say ignore them.

> —*John Steinbeck, 1902–1968, American novelist known for his
> sympathetic and realistic portrayal of migrant farm workers
> and working people in California. Two of his most notable
> works are* Of Mice and Men *and* The Grapes of Wrath.
> *He was awarded a Nobel Prize in 1962.*

Critics are like eunuchs in a harem. They're there every night, they see how it should be done every night, but they can't do it themselves.

> —*Brendan Behan, 1923–1964, Irish dramatist and poet
> who supported Irish nationalism and was twice
> convicted for terrorism. He was a famous drunk.*

—CYNICS—

Watch what people are cynical about, and one can often discover what they lack.

> —*Harry Emerson Fosdick, 1878–1969, American clergyman and author who favored liberal Protestant theology and was an advocate of pastoral counseling*

It takes a clever man to turn cynic, and a wise man to be clever enough not to.

> —*Fannie Hurst, 1889–1968, American novelist, playwright, and author of* Imitation of Life

—DECISION MAKING—

That action is best which procures the greatest happiness for the greatest numbers.

> —*Francis Hutcheson, 1694–1746, Scottish philosopher, educator, and author of* System of Moral Philosophy

When a man hasn't a good reason for doing a thing, he has a good reason for letting it alone.

> —*Walter Scott, 1771–1832, Scottish poet, novelist, historian, and biographer who wrote under various pseudonyms before putting his own name to his writing. He was known as "the Border Minstrel," "the Wizard of the North," and "the Great Magician." He is the author of the nine-volume* Life of Napoleon.

Next to knowing when to seize an opportunity, the most important thing in life is to know when to forgo an advantage.

—Benjamin Disraeli, 1804–1881, British prime minister, chancellor of exchequer, and first earl of Beaconsfield. Disraeli established Tory emphasis on strong foreign policy and became an intimate friend of Queen Victoria. He is the author of Sybil.

My method is different. I do not rush into actual work. When I get a new idea, I start at once building it up in my imagination, and make improvements and operate the device in my mind. . . . When I have gone so far as to embody everything in my invention, every possible improvement I can think of, and when I see no fault anywhere, I put into concrete form the final product of my brain.

—Nikola Tesla, 1856–1943, Croatian-born American physicist and electrical engineer who invented alternating current or AC power. He began his career in America working for Thomas Edison, but their disagreement over direct current versus alternating current led to Tesla's departure. Tesla worked as a ditch digger for a time before Western Union Telegraph took interest in his work. Near the end of his life, Tesla lived in a run-down New York City hotel room and spent much of his time feeding pigeons.

Do not choose to be wrong for the sake of being different.

—Herbert Louis Samuel, 1870–1963, British member of Parliament, high commissioner to Palestine, and postmaster general. As the leader of the Liberal Party, Samuel was responsible for the legislation that created juvenile courts in England. He is the author of Practical Ethics.

Whatever failures I have known, whatever errors I have committed, whatever follies I have witnessed in public and private life, have been the consequences of action without thought.

—Bernard M. Baruch, 1870–1965, chairman of the War Industries Board and U.S. representative to the United Nations Atomic Energy Commission. Baruch also worked in the brokerage business. He is known as an adviser to U.S. presidents and as a popular sage.

I have an absolute rule. I refuse to make a decision that somebody else can make. The first rule of leadership is to save yourself for the big decision. Don't allow your mind to become cluttered with the trivia. Don't let yourself become the issue.

> —*Richard M. Nixon, 1913–1994, thirty-seventh president of the United States. Nixon succeeded in withdrawing U.S. military forces from Vietnam and opening diplomatic relationships with China, but he was forced to resign from office as the result of his attempt to cover up the Watergate burglary.*

There are many ways to avoid mistakes, but the best way to sidestep the disasters is to be available. You don't have to make every decision, but you should always be accessible. If your people are smart they will keep you informed, and if you're informed, you're part of the decision. With that in place, it's easy for you to back your people and it eliminates second-guessing.

> —*T. Boone Pickens Jr., b. 1928, CEO of Mesa Petroleum who prides himself in not being part of the business "establishment" and often calls himself "a critic of entrenched managements and a vocal advocate of the stockholders"*

When faced with the tough decisions, gather all the data, weigh and analyze it, and take counsel from your most trusted advisers. Objectively weigh each factor you can grasp. Then, at the end of the day, when the facts are all considered, decide with your gut. Intuition separates the good leader from the great . . . the "feeling" of knowing the right thing to do. Learn to trust that "feeling."

> —*Leo J. "Lee" Baxter, b. 1946, American army major general who commanded the U.S. Army Field Artillery Center and Fort Sill*

—DECISIVENESS—

If I had to sum up in one word what makes a good manager I'd say decisiveness. You can use the fanciest computers to gather the numbers, but in the end you have to set a timetable and act.

> —Lee J. Iacocca, b. 1924, chairman of Chrysler Corporation who, against all odds, led Chrysler to a stunning turnaround in a time when virtually everyone else believed it would collapse

—DESTINY—

Destiny is not a matter of chance, it is a matter of choice; it is not a thing to be waited for, it is a thing to be achieved.

> —William Jennings Bryan, 1860–1925, American lawyer and politician known as "the Great Commoner." He was the prosecutor of evolutionist John T. Scopes in the famous "Scopes Monkey Trial," in which Scopes, a schoolteacher, stood trial for teaching evolution instead of creationism exclusively to his students. Bryan was also a three-time Democratic nominee for the U.S. presidency.

—DIGNITY—

No race can prosper till it learns that there is as much dignity in tilling a field as in writing a poem.

> —Booker T. Washington, 1856–1915, founder of Tuskegee Institute and leading commentator for African Americans. His support for segregation and his emphasis on vocational skills attracted criticism from other black leaders. He is the author of Up from Slavery.

No man who is occupied in doing a very difficult thing, and doing it very well, ever loses his self-respect.

> —*George Bernard Shaw, 1856–1950, Irish dramatist and writer.*
> Pygmalion *and Shaw's other most popular plays combine comedy with a questioning of conventional morality and thought. Shaw was a socialist and an active member in the Fabian Society. He received a Nobel Prize in 1925.*

—DISPOSITION—

The true gentleman is friendly but not familiar; the inferior man is familiar but not friendly. . . . The well-bred are dignified but not pompous; the ill-bred are pompous but not dignified.

> —*Confucius, 551–479 B.C., Chinese sage, philosopher, and father of Confucianism who was known as "Kong the Master"*

Civility costs nothing and buys everything.

> —*Mary Wortley Montagu, 1689–1762, English writer, poet, essayist, and feminist. Montagu taught herself Latin as a child. She accompanied her husband, Edward, on his ambassadorship to Constantinople. Although she was not a physician, Montagu introduced England to inoculation for smallpox, which she became aware of while in Turkey.*

Let us be of good cheer, however, remembering that the misfortunes hardest to bear are those that never come.

> —*James Russell Lowell, 1819–1891, American editor, poet, essayist, and diplomat. Lowell was the first editor of the* Atlantic Monthly.

Keep your fears to yourself, but share your courage with others.

>—Robert Louis Stevenson, 1850–1894, Scottish essayist, poet,
>and novelist. Stevenson was called to the Scottish bar but
>never practiced law. He is the author of Dr. Jekyll and
>Mr. Hyde, Kidnapped, and Treasure Island.

Imperturbable calm in the Commander is essential above all things.

>—Ian Hamilton, 1853–1947, Greek-born British army general.
>Hamilton served with distinction in the Boer Wars but led the
>disastrous Gallipoli Expedition and was relieved of his command.

Only the insane take themselves quite seriously.

>—Henry Maximilian Beerbohm, 1872–1956, English writer and
>caricaturist, nicknamed "the Incomparable Max." His novel, Zuleika
>Dobson, is a parody of life as an undergraduate at Oxford.

—DIVERSITY—

The traces of natural origin are a matter of expression even more than of feature.

>—Henry James, 1811–1882, American philosopher and author
>who was influenced by Fourierism—a system for reorganizing
>society into cooperative communities of small groups living in
>common. He is the author of Christianity: The Logic of Creation.

—DUTY—

Perhaps the most valuable result of all education is the ability to make yourself do the thing you have to do, when it ought to be done, whether you like it or not. It is the first lesson that ought to be learned.

> —*Thomas H. Huxley, 1825–1895, English biologist and surgeon. Huxley served as surgeon aboard H.M.S.* Rattlesnake, *sent to explore the southern seas. He was the foremost advocate in England of Darwin's theory of evolution and author of* Evolution and Ethics.

No man can always be right. So the struggle is to do one's best; to keep the brain and conscience clear; never to be swayed by unworthy motives or inconsequential reasons but to strive to unearth the basic factors involved, then do one's duty.

> —*Dwight D. Eisenhower, 1890–1969, thirty-fourth president of the United States. Eisenhower served in the army to the rank of general of the army. He was the supreme commander of the Allied Expeditionary Force in Europe during World War II and became supreme commander of NATO.*

—ENCOURAGEMENT—

Caution has its place, no doubt, but we cannot refuse our support to a serious venture which challenges the whole of the personality. If we oppose it—his daring and his aspirations—and should we succeed, we should only have stood in the way of invaluable experience which might have given a meaning to life. What would have happened if Paul had allowed himself to be talked out of his journey to Damascus?

> —*Carl Jung, 1875–1961, founder of analytic psychology and professor at the University of Zürich. Jung associated with Freud but differed with him on several concepts. Jung developed the concept of introversion and extroversion, as well as the theory of the collective unconscious and archetypes.*

Encouragement means hold others to high standards, recognizing their potential and not underestimating them. It can mean encouraging them, not just to become self-reliant and capable of achieving their goals, but to develop integrity and the character traits that accompany it. We not only can, but must, encourage others to be honest, fair, and reliable. Further, we must encourage them to exhibit self-discipline and to work hard, to be accountable, and to persevere at what they do in order to achieve their fullest potential.

> —*Dick DeVos, b. 1955, president of Amway Corporation, CEO of Orlando Magic NBA franchise, and author of* Rediscovering American Values. *Amway Corporation was one of the first multilevel marketing companies to have a significant impact in the marketplace. Many professionals (physicians, dentists, etc.) become Amway distributors as a way to build financial security should they become unable to perform in their professions.*

—ENDURANCE—

What cannot be cured must be endured.

> —*François Rabelais, c. 1483–1553, French writer, physician, and Benedictine priest. Rabelais's most noted novels, collectively known as* Gargantua and Pantagruel, *were first published under the pseudonym Alcofribas Nasier. These works are filled with racy humor and satire on events and doctrines of the day.*

Happy is he who learns to bear what he cannot change.

> —*Johann Christoph Friedrich von Schiller, 1759–1805, German historian, dramatist, poet, and author of* Wilhelm Tell

To endure is greater than to dare; to tire out hostile fortune; to be daunted by no difficulty; to keep heart when all have lost it; to go through intrigue spotless; to forgo even ambition when the end is gained—who can say this is not greatness?

> —*William Makepeace Thackeray, 1811–1863, English satirical novelist best known for his book* Vanity Fair

—ENEMIES—

Know the character of the enemy and their principal officers—whether they be rash or cautious, enterprising or timid, whether they fight on principle or from chance.

> —*Vegetius, fl. fourth century, Roman writer and author of* Epitoma rei militaris, *a treatise on military science that was very influential in the Middle Ages and later*

Pay attention to your enemies, for they are first to discover your mistakes.

> —*Antisthenes, c. 445–365 B.C., Greek philosopher who, along with Diogenes, is thought to be co-founder of the Cynic school*

Nothing is more dangerous than a friend without discretion; even a prudent enemy is preferable.

—*Jean de La Fontaine, 1621–1695, French poet, fabulist, and inspector of forests and waterways for the French government. La Fontaine was known for his wit, charm, facile morals, and absentmindedness.*

Your friends sometimes go to sleep, your enemies never do.

> —*Thomas Brackett Reed, 1839–1902, speaker of the
> U.S. House of Representatives who became known as
> "Czar Reed" for his ironclad control over the House*

A man cannot be too careful in the choice of his enemies.

> —*Oscar Wilde, 1854–1900, Irish dramatist, poet,
> author, and wit whose advocacy of "art for art's sake"
> is evident in his only novel,* The Picture of Dorian Gray

Our worst enemies here are not the ignorant and the simple, however cruel; our worst enemies are the intelligent and the corrupt.

> —*Graham Greene, 1904–1991, English novelist, dramatist,
> essayist, and screenwriter. Religious issues, especially
> Catholicism, were central to Greene's major novels.*

—ENTHUSIASTS—

It is unfortunate, considering that enthusiasm moves the world, that so few enthusiasts can be trusted to tell the truth.

> —*Arthur James Balfour, 1848–1930, British prime minister and first
> earl of Balfour. Balfour was responsible for the Balfour Declaration
> on Palestine and held several other positions in the British
> government, including serving as lord of the Admiralty.*

—ENTREPRENEURSHIP—

If you're going to be an entrepreneur, in a corporation or on your own, you should get a background in accounting. . . . In so many ways, analysis of a profit and loss statement or cash flow can be useful. . . . Any bottom line is reached by addition and subtraction and is read in dollar signs and decimal points.

—Victor Kiam, 1926–2001, CEO of Remington Products who once owned the New England Patriots National Football League franchise

Understand the art of management. Some entrepreneurs are so creative and committed to their business, they fail to delegate responsibilities to others, which can lead to failure. Hire talented employees who can carry out the nuts and bolts of your business. Let them share responsibility in the decision-making process. Keep an open mind, hear their ideas and suggestions first before you turn down their proposals. You can still oversee all aspects of your company while they are managing the business.

—Lillian Vernon, b. 1927, German-born American mail-order entrepreneur and founder and CEO of Lillian Vernon Corporation. One of America's most admired executives, Vernon founded her business in 1951 on her kitchen table using $2,000 of wedding gift money. She took out a $495 ad in Seventeen magazine offering a personalized belt and handbag. The ad brought in $32,000 in sales and her business was launched.

—EQUALITY—

All men are by nature equal, made all of the same earth by the same creator, and however we deceive ourselves, as dear to God is the poor peasant as the mighty prince.

—*Plato, 428–348 B.C., Greek philosopher, disciple of Socrates, and a teacher of Aristotle*

An earthly kingdom cannot exist without inequality of persons. Some must be free, some serfs, some rulers, some subjects.

—*Martin Luther, 1483–1546, founder of the Reformation and Protestantism. Luther preached the doctrine of salvation by faith rather than by works. He attacked the Roman Catholic Church over the sale of indulgences, nailing his written protest to the Wittenburg Chapel door.*

The true Republic: men, their rights and nothing more; women, their rights and nothing less.

—*Susan B. Anthony, 1820–1906, co-founder of the National Woman Suffrage Association and active in the temperance, abolitionist, and woman-suffrage movements of the day*

As long as you keep a person down, some part of you has to be down there to hold him down, so it means you cannot soar as you otherwise might.

—Marian Anderson, 1897–1993, American vocalist. Anderson made this observation during a concert at the Lincoln Memorial on Easter Sunday, April 9, 1939. Despite having to deal with overt racism from the beginning of her outstanding musical career, Anderson always conducted herself with great dignity and lived by the highest code of moral courage.

It is the mark of the cultured man that he is aware of the fact that equality is an ethical and not a biological principle.

> —*Ashley Montagu, 1905–1999, English-born American anthropologist, educator, and author. Born Israel Ehrenberg, Montagu is best known for his argument that aggression is not a natural human drive and for having discredited "race" as a specious and dangerous concept in the social sciences. He is the author of* Man's Most Dangerous Myth: The Fallacy of Race.

—ETHICS—

Prefer a loss to a dishonest gain; the one brings pain at the moment, the other for all time.

> —*Chilon, fl. sixth century B.C., Spartan who was one of five magistrates having power over the king*

When the end is lawful, the means are also lawful.

> —*Hermann Busenbaum, 1600–1668, German Jesuit priest and author of the popular* Medulla theologiae moralis, *a work which was later condemned for its sections on regicide (killing the monarch) and publicly burned by the Parliament of Toulouse*

The end must justify the means.

> —*Matthew Prior, 1664–1721, British diplomat, poet, and a close adviser to Queen Anne. Prior was secretary in the negotiations at Rijswijk. He took a leading part in framing the Treaty of Utrecht, which was called "Matt's Peace." He was impeached and imprisoned upon Queen Anne's death. While in prison, Prior wrote the long humorous poem* Progress of the Mind.

Great principles seldom escape working injustice in particular things.

—James Fenimore Cooper, 1789–1851, American novelist. Cooper lived the life of a country gentleman until his wife reputedly challenged him to write his first novel, Precaution. *Cooper wrote several more novels, the most popular being* The Last of the Mohicans.

A person who is fundamentally honest doesn't need a code of ethics. The Ten Commandments and the Sermon on the Mount are all the ethical code anybody needs.

—Harry S. Truman, 1884–1972, thirty-third president of the United States. Truman succeeded to the presidency on the death of Franklin D. Roosevelt. He always took full responsibility for his actions as was characterized by the sign he kept on his desktop that read "The Buck Stops Here." Truman ordered the atomic bombing of Hiroshima and Nagasaki, Japan, ending World War II.

It may be necessary temporarily to accept a lesser evil, but one must never label a necessary evil as good.

—Margaret Mead, 1901–1978, American anthropologist who spent considerable time in Samoa and New Guinea and wrote extensively on primitive cultures

—EXPECTATIONS—

All successful employers are stalking men who will do the unusual, men who think, men who attract attention by performing more than is expected of them.

> —*Charles M. Schwab, 1862–1939, founder, Bethlehem Steel Company. Schwab became the first president of U.S. Steel before he founded Bethlehem Steel.*

The only certain means of success is to render more and better service than is expected of you, no matter what your task may be.

> —*Og Mandino, 1923–1996, American insurance salesman, motivational speaker, and author of* The Greatest Salesman in the World. *Mandino received the Distinguished Flying Cross for his gallantry as an army aviation navigator during World War II.*

—EXPERIENCE—

There are many truths of which the full meaning cannot be realized until personal experience has brought it home.

> —*John Stuart Mill, 1806–1873, English philosopher, economist, and writer best known for his book* On Liberty

We should be careful to get out of an experience only the wisdom that is in it—and stop there; lest we be like the cat that sits down on a hot stove-lid. She will never sit down on a hot stove-lid again—and that is well; but also she will never sit down on a cold one any more.

> —*Mark Twain, 1835–1910, American novelist and humorist. Mark Twain is the pseudonym of Samuel Langhorne Clemens. His most widely read works are* The Adventures of Tom Sawyer *and* The Adventures of Huckleberry Finn.

Experience is valuable only if it is imbued with meaning from which one can draw salient conclusions. Otherwise, experience becomes imprisoning.

> —*Barry R. McCaffrey, b. 1942, American army general who was commander-in-chief of the U.S. Southern Command in Panama before being appointed as director of the White House Office of National Drug Control Policy. He also served as a member of the National Security Council and the Cabinet Council on Counternarcotics.*

—FAILURE—

He who has never failed somewhere, that man can not be great.

> —*Herman Melville, 1819–1891, American novelist and short-story writer whose experiences on a whaling ship provided him insight for several of his novels, the most notable being* Moby Dick

I don't know the key to success. But the key to failure is trying to please everybody.

> —*Bill Cosby, b. 1937, American comedian, actor, and author. As costar of* I Spy, *Cosby was the first African American to star in a weekly television drama. He was also the star of* The Cosby Show, *which was one of the most successful sitcoms in television history. Cosby is the author of* Fatherhood.

—FAME—

Fame has also this great drawback, that if we pursue it we must direct our lives in such a way as to please the fancy of men, avoiding what they dislike and seeking what is pleasing to them.

> —*Baruch Spinoza, 1632–1677, Dutch philosopher who was the most prominent rational pantheism philosopher. He considered "God or nature" as a single infinite substance, with mind and matter being two incommensurable ways of conceiving the one reality. His views got him excommunicated from the synagogue, and he ended up grinding lenses to support himself.*

Never esteem men on account of their riches or their station. Respect goodness, find it where you may.

> —*William Cobbett, 1763–1835, English journalist, essayist, editor, and author of* Advice to Young Men. *Cobbett taught himself grammar and composition while serving in the British army and later wrote in vigorous prose. He wrote under the pseudonym Peter Porcupine, published* Porcupine's Gazette, *and edited the* Political Register. *He was the leader of a small number of radical thinkers and was imprisoned for denouncing flogging of militiamen.*

Avoid shame but do not seek glory—nothing so expensive as glory.

> —*Sydney Smith, 1771–1845, English publisher, clergyman, essayist, wit, and co-founder of the* Edinburgh Review. *Smith was known for his sound political reasoning spiced with wit. He created the character Mrs. Partington, who was later made famous by American humorist Benjamin Penhallow Shillaber in* Life and Sayings of Mrs. Partington.

Beware of over-great pleasure in being popular or ever beloved.

> —*Margaret Fuller, 1810–1850,*
> *American writer and feminist.*
> *Fuller was a supporter of Emerson.*
> *Her book* Women in the 19th Century
> *is the earliest work of American*
> *feminist writing.*

How glorious it is—and how painful—to be an exception.

—Alfred de Musset, 1810–1857, French writer and poet.
Musset wrote precocious poetry that was romantic
but leavened by ironic, flippant wit.

It would be a good thing if man concerned himself more with the history of his nature than with the history of his deeds.

—Friedrich Hebbel, 1813–1863, German poet and playwright
who wrote realistic, psychological tragedies involving
Hegelian concepts of history and moral values

It is a mark of many famous people that they cannot part with their brightest hour.

—Lillian Hellman, 1905–1984, American dramatist.
Hellman's plays are melodramatic but intelligent and well
crafted. Her first drama, The Children's Hour, *concerns the*
devastating effects of a child's malicious charge of
lesbianism against two of her teachers. Hellman also
wrote The Little Foxes.

—FATE—

A man's character is his fate.

> —*Heracleitus, c. 540–480 B.C., Greek philosopher known in later ages as "the weeping philosopher." Heracleitus held that fire is the principal element of all things.*

I often feel, and ever more deeply I realize, that fate and character are the same conception.

> —*Novalis, 1772–1801, German poet. Novalis is the pseudonym of Friedrich Leopold von Hardenberg, a leader of early romanticists in Germany.*

There is no inevitability in history except as men make it.

> —*Felix Frankfurter, 1882–1965, U.S. Supreme Court justice and adviser to President Franklin D. Roosevelt. Frankfurter taught at Harvard Law School and helped found the American Civil Liberties Union. He was a leading exponent of the doctrine of judicial self-restraint.*

Nothing is inevitable until it happens.

> —*A. J. P. Taylor, 1906–1990, English historian and author. Alan John Percivale Taylor aroused passionate hostility with his revisionist book* The Origins of the Second World War.

—FAVORS—

Men are never attached to you by favors.

—Napoleon Bonaparte, 1769–1821, Corsican-born French army general and emperor of France. Napoleon made widespread changes to France's government and educational system and established the Legion of Merit. Napoleon was one of the greatest military commanders in history but was nevertheless defeated by Wellington at the Battle of Waterloo in 1815, which led to his abdication as emperor and the end of the Napoleonic wars.

Never let your inferiors do you a favor—it will be very costly.

—H. L. Mencken, 1880–1956, American journalist and literary and social critic. Henry Louis Mencken was on the staff of the Baltimore Morning Herald, *the* Baltimore Evening Herald, *the* Baltimore Sun, *and the* Baltimore Evening Sun. *He was also contributing editor to* The Nation.

—FEEDBACK—

There are plenty of people to whom the crucial problems of their lives never get presented in terms they understand.

—John Jay Chapman, 1862–1933, American lawyer, essayist, and dramatist. Chapman is best known for his essays and as author of Causes and Consequences.

—FOCUS—

Concentrate all your thoughts upon the work at hand. The sun's rays do not burn until brought to a focus.

—Alexander Graham Bell, 1847–1922, Scottish-born American scientist and inventor. Bell patented the telephone and produced the first intelligible telephone transmission multiplexing system. He founded the journal Science.

—FORCE—

Where force is necessary, one should make use of it boldly, resolutely, and right to the end. But it is as well to know the limitations of force; to know where to blend force with maneuver, assault with conciliation.

> *—Leon Trotsky, 1879–1940, Russian Communist leader, revolutionary, author, Soviet commissar for foreign affairs, and commissar for war. Born Lev Davidovich Bronstein, Trotsky became a close ally of Lenin and created the Red Army. He is the author of* The Defense of Terrorism *and* History of the Russian Revolution. *Stalin banished Trotsky from Russia, but Trotsky found haven in Mexico, where he lived until his murder in 1940.*

—FORGIVENESS—

We read that we ought to forgive our enemies; but we do not read that we ought to forgive our friends.

> *—Cosimo de' Medici, 1389–1464, Italian statesman, financier, and philanthropist. Medici helped establish Florence as the center of new learning.*

He who has not forgiven an enemy has never yet tasted one of the most sublime enjoyments of life.

> *—Johann Kaspar Lavater, 1741–1801, Swiss poet, mystic, and clergyman. A Protestant pastor, Lavater was the founder of physiognomy, which is the art of discovering character and temperament from outward appearance.*

—FREEDOM—

No man is wholly free. He is a slave to wealth, or to fortune, or the laws, or the people restrain him from acting according to his will alone.

> —*Euripides, 484–406 B.C., Greek tragic dramatist.*
> *Euripides ranks with Aeschylus and Sophocles as one*
> *of the greatest Greek tragic poets. He wrote the plays*
> The Trojan Women, Helen, Electra, *and* Cyclops.

A man's worst difficulties begin when he is able to do as he likes.

> —*T. H. Huxley, 1825–1895, English biologist, surgeon, educator,*
> *and philosopher. Thomas Henry Huxley was the leading*
> *supporter of Darwin's theory of evolution. Huxley also*
> *coined the term* agnostic *to describe his religious beliefs.*

Liberty means freedom to do not what one wants to do, but what one ought to do.

> —*John Emerich Edward Dalberg, 1834–1902, British noble,*
> *historian, and educator. Dalberg is popularly known as "Lord Acton."*
> *He was a professor at Cambridge and the leader of English liberal*
> *Roman Catholics opposing the dogma of papal infallibility.*

—GENIUS—

If we are to have genius we must put up with the inconvenience of genius, and that the world will never do; it wants geniuses, but would like them just like other people.

—George Augustus Moore, 1852–1933, Irish author. Moore studied art in Paris with Manet, Degas, Renoir, and Monet but left art to become a writer. He wrote several realistic novels, including Esther Waters, *helped establish the Abbey Theatre, and, with Edward Martyn and Y. B. Yeats, led the Irish literary revival of the day.*

—GOALS—

There are two things to aim at in life; first, to get what you want; and after that, to enjoy it. Only the wisest of mankind achieve the second.

—Logan Pearsall Smith, 1865–1946, American author best known for Reperusals *and* Re-collections

Injustice, poverty, slavery, ignorance—these may be cured by reform or revolution. But men do not live only by fighting evils. They live by positive goals, individual and collective, a vast variety of them, seldom predictable, at times incompatible.

—Isaiah Berlin, 1909–1997, Latvian-born English philosopher, educator, and historian of ideas. Berlin is noted for his pluralist views and considered to be one of the most prominent twentieth-century philosophers. He was the first president of Oxford University's Wolfson College.

A goal is an enemy to be conquered with a battle strategy and the commitment of a warrior. The leadership process is founded on resolve and commitment. There is no success in giving up.

—*Tom Garriga, b. 1945, president, Tang Wei Martial Arts Institute. Garriga has black-belt ranking in twenty-two martial art styles, is a fifth step (master) of Wu Ji Chyuan Fa, and is a ninth-degree black belt in American Kenpo Karate.*

—GOSSIP—

Whoever gossips will gossip about you.

—Spanish proverb

How seldom a fact is accurately stated; how almost invariably when a story passes through the mind of a third person [it is] . . . little better than a falsehood; and this, too, though the narrator be the most truth-seeking person in existence.

—Nathaniel Hawthorne, 1804–1864, American novelist and short-story writer. Much of Hawthorne's writing explores guilt, sin, and morality. He is the author of The House of Seven Gables.

Gossip is a sort of smoke that comes from the dirty tobacco-pipes of those who diffuse it: It proves nothing but the bad taste of the smoker.

—George Eliot, 1819–1880, English novelist. George Eliot is the pseudonym of Mary Ann Evans. She wrote several realistic novels, including Silas Marner. *Her London home served as a center of Victorian intellectual and literary life.*

The thing from which the world suffers just now more than from any other evil is not the assertion of falsehood, but the endless and irrepressible repetition of half-truths.

—Gilbert Keith Chesterton, 1874–1936, English journalist, critic, writer, and author of What's Wrong with the World?

Ah, well, the truth is always one thing, but in a way it's the other thing, the gossip, that counts. It shows where people's hearts be.

—Paul Scott, 1920–1978, English writer. Scott served in India during World War II and later most of his novels in India. He is the author of The Alien Sky.

—HABITS—

Habits change into character.

—Ovid, 43 B.C.–17 A.D., Roman poet. Educated for the practice of law, Ovid preferred writing as his career. He wrote many love poems, but his chief work was Metamorphoses, *a narrative poem recounting legends involving miraculous transformations of forms from the creation to the time of Julius Caesar.*

There is no more miserable human being than one for whom nothing is habitual but indecision.

—William James, 1842–1910, American psychologist, educator, philosopher, and writer, and one of the founders of pragmatism

—HAPPINESS—

I used to think it was great to disregard happiness, to press on to a high goal, careless, disdainful of it. But now I see that there is nothing so great as to be capable of happiness.

—Anne Burrow Gilchrist, 1828–1885, English writer. A Victorian woman, Gilchrist nevertheless took delight in what so many others found "vulgar" in Whitman's verse. She wrote An Englishwoman's Estimate of Walt Whitman *and became close friends with him. She was well known and highly respected in literary circles of the day.*

—HONESTY—

Honesty is a good thing but it is not profitable to its possessor unless it is kept under control.

> —*Don Marquis, 1878–1937, American journalist and humorist who edited the* Uncle Remus's Magazine *and was a journalist for the* New York Sun *and the* New York Tribune. *He wrote a column called "The Sun Dial," in which he introduced Mehitabel the Cat, Archy the Cockroach, and other characters.*

—HOPE—

In great straits and when hope is small, the boldest counsels are the safest.

> —*Titus Livius Livy, 59 B.C.–17 A.D., Roman historian. Under the patronage of Emperor Augustus, Livy wrote* The Annals of the Roman People, *which consists of 142 books and provides the history of Rome from its foundation to the death of Drusus.*

When hope is taken away from a people moral degeneration follows swiftly after.

> —*Pearl S. Buck, 1892–1973, American novelist and author of* The Good Earth, *which earned her a Pulitzer Prize in 1931. Buck also wrote under the pseudonym John Sedges. She was awarded a Nobel Prize in 1938.*

There are no hopeless situations; there are only men who have grown hopeless about them.

> —*Clare Boothe Luce, 1903–1987, American dramatist, author, editor, Republican politician, and diplomat. The author of the highly successful play* The Women, *Luce was a war correspondent during World War II. After serving in the U.S. House of Representatives, Luce became the first American woman ambassador to a major country when President Eisenhower appointed her as ambassador to Italy.*

—HUMAN NATURE—

Never in this world can hatred be stilled by hatred; it will be stilled only by non-hatred—this is the law Eternal.

> —*Buddha, c. 563–483 B.C., founder of Buddhism and sage of Sakyas. Born Siddhartha Gautama, Buddha achieved his enlightenment while meditating under a banyon tree at Buddha Gaya. He taught the doctrines of the Four Noble Truths and the chain of causation.*

Nothing is so easy as to deceive one's self; for what we wish, we readily believe.

> —*Demosthenes, c. 384–322 B.C., Greek orator, leading speaker in the Athenian assembly, and leader of the popular party. His criticism of Philip of Macedon led to his exile. After the death of Alexander, he was recalled to Athens, where he was later condemned to death but committed suicide before he could be executed. Demosthenes was the greatest of Greek orators.*

Men are more ready to offend one who desires to be beloved than one who wishes to be feared.

> —*Niccolò Machiavelli, 1469–1527, Italian statesman, philosopher, and author whose leadership masterpiece,* The Prince (Il Principe), *was the first book to address how leaders* really *gain and maintain power*

A fool knows more in his own house than a wise body in another man's.

> —*Miguel de Cervantes, 1547–1616, Spanish novelist and soldier. Cervantes was captured by Algerian pirates, enslaved, and held for ransom. Although author of the classic* Don Quixote, *he suffered poverty in his life.*

People are always much more inclined to prefer present interest to the distant and remote.

> —*David Hume, 1711–1776, Scottish philosopher, historian, and diplomat. Hume served in the British embassy in Paris and was undersecretary of state. His philosophy is marked by its skepticism and empiricism, restricting the limits of human knowledge. He is the author of* Philosophical Essays Concerning Human Understanding.

A man in the wrong may more easily be convinced than one half right.

> —*Ralph Waldo Emerson, 1803–1882, American philosopher and poet. Emerson evolved the concept of transcendentalism, which finds expression in his essay* Nature.

Men do not change their characters by uniting with one another, nor does their patience in the presence of obstacles increase their strength.

> —*Alexis de Tocqueville, 1805–1859, French politician, historian, and author of* Democracy in America

It is a trick among the dishonest to offer sacrifices that are not needed, or not possible, to avoid making those that are required.

> —*Ivan Aleksandrovich Goncharov, 1812–1891, Russian civil servant and novelist whose novel* Oblomov *is one of the greatest and most typical works of Russian realism*

The trouble with people is not that they don't know but that they know so much that ain't so.

—*Josh Billings, 1818–1885, American humor writer. Henry Wheeler Shaw, who wrote under the pseudonym Josh Billings, worked as an auctioneer and real estate dealer before becoming a writer. He contributed to* Century *magazine under the pseudonym Uncle Esek. He relied heavily on deliberate misspelling, as in "Essa on the Muel" ("Essay on the Mule").*

One of the greatest pains to human nature is the pain of a new idea.

—*Walter Bagehot, 1826–1877, English economist, journalist,*
author, and pioneer in applying sociology and evolutionary
thought to business and economic topics

There are four kinds of people in the world: those in love, the ambitious, the observers, and the stupid. The most happy are the stupid.

—*Hippolyte-Adolphe Taine, 1828–1893, French philosopher*
and professor at the École des Beaux-Arts. Taine was
a leading exponent of French positivism and applied
scientific method to the study of humanities.

There are very honest people who do not think they have had a bargain unless they have cheated a merchant.

—*Anatole France, 1844–1924, French author. Anatole France*
is the pseudonym of Jacques-Anatole-François Thibault.
He was awarded a Nobel Prize in 1921.

The third-rate mind is only happy when it is thinking with the majority. The second-rate mind is only happy when it is thinking with the minority. The first-class mind is only happy when it is thinking.

—*A. A. Milne, 1882–1956, English author. Alan Alexander Milne*
wrote stories and poems for children. He created the character
Winnie-the-Pooh for his son, Christopher Robin.

It is not neurotic to have conflicts. . . . Conflicts with ourselves are an integral part of human life.

> —*Karen Horney, 1885–1952, German-born American psychoanalyst. Horney was expelled from the New York Psychoanalytic Institute for her critique of Freudian practices.*

We are all inclined to judge ourselves by our ideals; others by their acts.

> —*Harold George Nicolson, 1886–1968, British member of Parliament, delegate to the Paris peace talks, and member of the embassy in Berlin. Nicolson is the author of several biographies, including* Tennyson, Byron, *and* King George V. *He also wrote* Good Behaviour *and* Age of Reason.

There are no desperate situations, there are only desperate people.

> —*Heinz Wilhelm Guderian, 1888–1954, German army general. Fluent and hot-tempered, Guderian was the creator of the German army's* Panzerwaffe *and blitzkrieg tactics. He was relieved from duty as Germany's chief of army staff over disagreements with Hitler. Guderian became a prisoner of war after surrendering to the U.S. army in May 1945. He was later sent to Nuremberg but was not tried for war crimes, as there was no evidence that he participated in the Holocaust.*

Great innovators and original thinkers and artists attract the wrath of mediocrities as lightning rods draw the flashes.

> —*Theodor Reik, 1888–1969, Austrian-born founder of the National Psychological Association for Psychoanalysis. Reik was one of Freud's earliest and brightest students. He is the author of* Listening with the Third Ear.

Consistency is contrary to nature, contrary to life. The only completely consistent people are dead.

> —*Aldous Huxley, 1894–1963, English-born English and*
> *American novelist and essayist. Huxley wrote about*
> *his experiences with psychedelic drugs while living*
> *in California in his book* The Doors of Perception.
> *But he is best known for* Brave New World.

A commander should have a profound understanding of human nature, the knack of smoothing out troubles, the power of winning affection while communicating energy, and the capacity for ruthless determination where required by circumstances. He needs to generate an electrifying current, and to keep a cool head in applying it.

> —*Basil Henry Liddell Hart, 1895–1970, British military*
> *historian, strategist, and author. Liddell Hart developed*
> *principles of mobile warfare used by both the Allied*
> *and Axis armies during World War II.*

People cannot remain good unless good is expected of them.

> —*Bertolt Brecht, 1898–1956, German playwright and poet.*
> *Brecht was a Marxist and fled his fear of the Nazis by fleeing*
> *to Denmark, Sweden, Finland, and the United States.*
> *He resettled in East Germany after World War II. Symbolists*
> *and expressionists heavily influenced his writing.*

HUMOR

Humor is one of God's most marvelous gifts. Humor gives us smiles, laughter, and gaiety. Humor reveals the roses and hides the thorns. Humor makes our heavy burdens light and smooths down the rough spots in our pathways. Humor endows us with the capacity to clarify the obscure, to simplify the complex, to deflate the pompous, to chastise the arrogant, to point a moral, and to adorn a tale.

—Sam J. Erwin Jr., 1896–1985, American Democratic politician, lawyer, and author. As a U.S. senator from North Carolina, Erwin won the respect of his colleagues by his unequivocal condemnation of Senator Joseph McCarthy's practices, which was a major factor in McCarthy's censure by the Senate. He also played a key role in the Watergate hearings, which eventually led to President Richard Nixon's resignation.

—IDEALISM—

All the Utopias will come to pass only when we grow wings and all people are converted to angels.

—Fyodor Mikhaylovich Dostoyevski, 1821–1881, Russian novelist and soldier. Dostoyevski resigned from the army to take up writing. He was convicted of conspiracy but reprieved from execution and did four years of hard labor at a Siberian prison camp. His novels were in-depth studies of people and their search for faith, meaning, and truth. He is the author of Crime and Punishment.

Idealism increases in direct proportion to one's distance from the problem.

—John Galsworthy, 1867–1933, English novelist and dramatist primarily known as the author of The Forsythe Saga, *a series of novels that were adapted for television. He received a Nobel Prize in 1932.*

Idealism is fine, but as it approaches reality the cost becomes prohibitive.

> —*William F. Buckley Jr., b. 1925, American journalist, author,*
> *publisher, and commentator. Buckley is the founder of*
> National Review *and hosted television's* Firing Line.

—IDLENESS—

Iron rusts from disuse, stagnant water loses its purity, and in cold weather becomes frozen; even so does inaction sap the vigors of the mind.

> —*Leonardo da Vinci, 1452–1519, Italian painter, sculptor,*
> *architect, musician, engineer, and scientist. Da Vinci is perhaps*
> the *supreme example of Renaissance genius and one of the*
> *greatest minds in history. He employed scientific precision and*
> *consummate artistry in his paintings, which include such*
> *masterpieces as* St. John the Baptist, Madonna of the Rocks, *and*
> the Last Supper. *Da Vinci was highly regarded in his day and*
> *became a close friend of Niccolò Machiavelli.*

A man is not idle because he is absorbed in thought. There is a visible labor and there is an invisible labor.

> —*Victor Hugo, 1802–1885, French romantic poet, dramatist,*
> *novelist, and politician. Hugo is considered one of the greatest*
> *poets of his day and is the author of* Les Misérables. *His*
> *father was a general under Napoleon; however, Hugo was*
> *banished from France for a time because of his opposition to*
> *Napoleon III. After a triumphant return to Paris, Hugo was*
> *elected to the National Assembly and the senate and lived*
> *out his life in public veneration and acclaim.*

—INDIFFERENCE—

We know what happens to people who stay in the middle of the road. They get run over.

—Aneurin Bevan, 1897–1960, British Labour politician, coal miner, and trade unionist. He was also a member of Parliament and minister of health. Bevan was the leader of the Labour Party's left wing and was briefly expelled from the party for insubordination. He favored British diplomatic neutralism and nuclear disarmament.

—INDIVIDUALITY—

While the individual man is an insoluble puzzle, in the aggregate, he becomes a mathematical certainty. You can never foretell what any one man will do, but you can always predict with precision what an average number of men will be up to. Individuals vary but percentages remain constant.

—Arthur Conan Doyle, 1859–1930, Scottish-born English physician, soldier, and author of The Sign of Four. This observation of Doyle's was a line delivered by the most famous character of his creation, Detective Sherlock Holmes. Holmes first appeared in A Study in Scarlet, for which Doyle was paid the sum of £25.

What an individual thinks or feels as success is unique with him. In our experience we have found that each individual has a different meaning of, and attitude toward, what constitutes success. Therefore, a human being cannot be typified or classified.

—Alfred Adler, 1870–1937, Austrian-born Austrian and American psychoanalyst. A student and an associate of Freud, Adler believed society and culture contribute to mental illness and introduced the concept of inferiority complex. Adler established the first child-guidance clinic in Vienna before immigrating to the United States, where he became known as "the father of individual psychology."

—INITIATIVE—

We will either find a way or make one.

> —*Hannibal, 247–183? B.C., Carthaginian general who led an army across the Alps to engage in a fifteen-year war against the Romans on Italian soil during the second Punic War. As a military leader, Hannibal is in the same elite league as Alexander the Great, Napoleon Bonaparte, and Julius Caesar.*

There are two kinds of men who never amount to much: those who cannot do what they are told, and those who can do nothing else.

> —*Cyrus H. Curtis, 1850–1933, CEO, Curtis Publishing. Curtis established the* Tribune and Farmer *magazine and* Ladies' Home Journal. *Curtis Publishing also published* The Country Gentleman *and the* Saturday Evening Post *and purchased the* New York Evening Post, *the* Philadelphia Enquirer, *and other newspapers.*

It's the job that's never started that takes longest to finish.

> —*J. R. R. Tolkien, 1892–1973, South African–born English novelist and literary scholar who is best known for his Middle Earth fantasy adventures* The Hobbit, The Lord of the Rings, *and* The Silmarillion

If you want to catch beasts you don't see every day,
You have to go places quite out-of-the-way.
You have to go places no others can get to.
You have to get cold and you have to get wet, too.

> —*Theodor Seuss Geisel, 1904–1991, American author and illustrator. This observation of Geisel's is the musing of Gerald McGrew, the principal character in* If I Ran the Zoo. *Geisel wrote and illustrated forty-four world-famous books for children using the pen name Dr. Seuss. His first book,* And to Think that I Saw It on Mulberry Street, *was rejected by forty-three publishers.*

Good leaders don't wait for official blessing to try things out. They're prudent, not reckless. But they realize a fact of life in most organizations: If you ask enough people for permission, you'll inevitably come up against someone who believes his job is to say "no." So the moral is, don't ask. Less effective middle managers endorse the sentiment, "If I haven't explicitly been told 'yes,' I can't do it," whereas the good ones believe, "If I haven't explicitly been told 'no,' I can." There's a world of difference between the two points of view.

—Colin Powell, b. 1937, American army general, chairman of the Joint Chiefs of Staff, and U.S. secretary of state. Powell gained fame through the role he played in the conduct of the Gulf War. He is the first African American to serve either as chairman of the Joint Chiefs of Staff or U.S. secretary of state. He also served as chairman of America's Promise.

—INSIGHT—

Discovery consists of seeing what everybody has seen and thinking what nobody has thought.

> —*Albert von Nagyrapolt Szent-Györgyi, 1893–1986,*
> *Hungarian-born American biochemist. Szent-Györgyi discovered*
> *ascorbic acid, which is commonly known as vitamin C.*

—INSPIRATION—

You can't wait for inspiration. You have to go after it with a club.

> —*Jack London, 1876–1916, American novelist and short-story writer.*
> *Before establishing himself as a writer, London was a sailor,*
> *waterfront loafer, and hobo, and he joined the Klondike gold rush.*
> *London wrote fifty books, including* The Call of the Wild.

A true leader inspires others to lead themselves.

> —*Ari D. Kaplan, b. 1970, CEO, PocketDBA Systems.*
> *Kaplan is widely recognized as one of the world's*
> *leading information-technology gurus.*

—INTEGRITY—

Ensuring integrity at our firm has always been a top priority and will continue to be.

> —*E. Stanley O'Neal, b. 1951, president and COO, Merrill Lynch,*
> *from* USA Today, *July 25, 2001. O'Neal, whose grandfather*
> *was born a slave, is set to become the first African American*
> *to head Wall Street's largest brokerage firm.*

—INTELLECTUALS—

I think I detect today a certain public skepticism when intellectuals stand up to preach to us, a growing tendency among ordinary people to dispute the right of academics, writers and philosophers, eminent though they may be, to tell us how to behave and conduct our affairs. The belief seems to be spreading that intellectuals are no wiser as mentors, or worthier as exemplars, than the witch doctors or priests of old. I share that skepticism. A dozen people picked at random on the street are at least as likely to offer sensible views on moral and political matters as a cross-section of the intelligentsia. . . . Above all, we must at all times remember what intellectuals habitually forget: that people matter more than concepts and must come first. The worst of all despotisms is the heartless tyranny of ideas.

—Paul Johnson, b. 1928, English biographer, historian, author, editor, and journalist, from Intellectuals. *In addition to being a prolific writer, Johnson has made more than forty television films.*

—INTERDEPENDENCE—

There are many objects of great value to man which cannot be attained by unconnected individuals, but must be attained, if attained at all, by association.

—Daniel Webster, 1782–1852, U.S. secretary of state, U.S. representative, and U.S. senator. One of America's greatest orators, Webster gained fame for his constitutional speeches.

Troops should not be encouraged to foster a spirit of jealousy and unjust detraction towards other arms of the service, where all are mutually dependent and mutually interested, with functions differing in character but not in importance.

—J. E. B. Stuart, 1833–1864, American Confederate Army general who was the Confederacy's most highly regarded cavalry commander

If you want a man to be for you, never let him feel he is dependent on you. Make him feel you are in some way dependent on him.

—George C. Marshall, 1880–1959, army chief of staff, U.S. secretary of state, and U.S. secretary of defense. Marshall devised the European Recovery Plan, known as the Marshall Plan, for helping European countries rebuild after World War II. He received a Nobel Prize in 1953.

There isn't a person alive who is not afraid of being isolated. In our daily lives we might come across a few bullies who like to boast, "What am I afraid of? I don't need to please anybody. I can fend for myself and don't need anything from anybody." But if you really isolate such a person, he too would be afraid because he knows that he isn't some king or mighty tiger that can roam about on his own, but is rooted in society and relies on it for his very existence.

—Wei Jingsheng, b. 1951, Chinese human-rights activist. Jingsheng was a Red Guard before becoming an outspoken critic of the Chinese government's policies and an advocate of human rights. His book The Courage to Stand Alone *was written while he was a political prisoner. He received the European Parliament's Sakharov Prize for Freedom of Thought in 1996.*

—JUSTICE—

The strictest justice is sometimes the greatest injustice.

—Terence, c. 186–159 B.C., Carthaginian-born Roman playwright.
Terence was taken to Rome as a slave of a Roman senator.
He is considered the master of Latin comedy.

Everyone suffers wrongs for which there is no remedy.

—Edgar Watson Howe, 1853–1937, American journalist,
editor, and author. Known as "the Sage of Potato Hill,"
Howe was a master of homely wisdom.

As long as the world shall last there will be wrongs, and if no man objected and no man rebelled, those wrongs would last forever.

—Clarence Darrow, 1857–1938, American lawyer and
writer. Darrow was one of the great defense lawyers of his
day. He defended John T. Scopes, who was accused of
violating Tennessee law for teaching evolution in a public
school, in the famous "Scopes Monkey Trial."

—LOYALTY—

Rome owed much of her patriotism to her many festivals.

> —*Jean Paul, 1763–1825, German novelist. Jean Paul is the pseudonym of Jean Paul Friedrich Richter, who wrote romances as well as patriotic, philosophical, and political works.*

Unless you can find some sort of loyalty, you cannot find unity and peace in your active living.

> —*Josiah Royce, 1855–1916, American philosopher, author, and professor at Harvard University. Royce studied under William James and Charles S. Peirce. He developed a philosophy of idealism that places individuality and will ahead of intellect.*

Nothing knits man to man like the frequent passage from hand to hand of cash.

> —*Walter Sickert, 1860–1942, German-born English painter who was a pupil of Whistler and influenced by Degas and the neo-impressionists. He is best known for his paintings of London-music-hall interiors.*

You've got to give loyalty down, if you want loyalty up.

> —*Donald T. Regan, b. 1918, president of Merrill Lynch, U.S. secretary of the treasury, and White House chief of staff. As the result of criticism of his role in "Irangate," Regan was forced to resign as White House chief of staff.*

—LUCK—

There is a play of possibilities and probabilities, of good luck and bad luck, which permeates every thread, great or small, of the web of human activity.

> —*Carl von Clausewitz, 1780–1831, Prussian general, military theorist, and author of* On War

I don't know anything about luck. I've never banked on it, and I'm afraid of people who do. Luck to me is something else: hard work—and realizing what is opportunity and what isn't.

> —*Lucille Ball, 1911–1989, American comedian and actor who played "Lucy," one of television's best-loved characters, in* I Love Lucy, The Lucy Show, *and* Here's Lucy

I think the harder you work, the more luck you have.

> —*R. David Thomas, b. 1932, founder and CEO, Wendy's International Inc. Thomas owned a Kentucky Fried Chicken franchise before starting Wendy's Old-Fashioned Hamburgers. He has appeared in more television commercials than any other business executive.*

Some luck lies in not getting what you thought you wanted by getting what you have, which once you have got it you may be smart enough to see is what you would have wanted had you known.

> —*Garrison Keillor, b. 1942, American writer and radio entertainer who created the radio program* A Prairie Home Companion *and is author of* Wobegon Boy

—MANAGEMENT—

Without supplies neither a general nor a soldier is good for anything.

—Clearchus of Sparta, fl. fifth century B.C., Spartan politician, general, and governor of Byzantium

Generally, management of the many is the same as management of the few. It is a matter of organization.

—Sun-tzu, fl. fourth century B.C., Chinese military strategist, writer, and reputed author of Ping-fa (The Art of War), *which is one of the earliest-known treatises on war and strategy. This book's emphasis on the political aspects of war continues to influence modern-day leaders.*

It is frequently a misfortune to have very brilliant men in charge of affairs; they expect too much of ordinary men.

—Thucydides, c. 460–400 B.C., Greek politician who led the aristocratic party after the death of Cimon. He became a critic of Pericles, a political blunder that resulted in his being ostracized and stripped of power.

Those who apply themselves too closely to little things often become incapable of great things.

—François de La Rochefoucauld, 1613–1680, French moralist. As a soldier, La Rochefoucauld was wounded in the siege of Paris. His literary fame stems from Réflexions ou sentences et maximes morales, *which was first published anonymously.*

There is no indispensable man.

—Woodrow Wilson, 1856–1924, twenty-eighth president of the United States. Wilson was the governor of New Jersey before being elected president. As president, he established the Federal Trade Commission and signed the 18th Amendment ratifying Prohibition.

Surround yourself with the best people you can find, delegate authority, and don't interfere as long as the policy you've decided upon is being carried out.

—Ronald Reagan, b. 1911, actor and fortieth president of the United States. Perhaps the greatest legacy of Reagan's presidency is the role he played in the demise of Soviet communism that led to the end of the Cold War and the destruction of the Berlin Wall—the only such wall in history built to keep people in rather than protect them from outsiders.

If you have something that doesn't fit with your operations, sell it. Don't try to get top dollar for it. You more than make up for any difference you might get by being able to concentrate on the business you should be concentrating on.

> —*Sanford I. Weill, b. 1933, CEO, Citigroup. Weill was also CEO of Travelers Group, president of American Express, and CEO of Fireman's Fund Insurance Companies. A self-made man, Weill is one of the most highly regarded financial-services executives in the world.*

If you pick the right people and give them the opportunity to spread their wings—and put compensation as a carrier behind it—you almost don't have to manage them.

> —*John F. "Jack" Welch Jr., b. 1935, CEO, General Electric. Welch is regarded as one of the most effective business managers in the world.*

—MEETINGS—

But sometimes you go to meetings where the purpose is to get your "input" on something. This is very serious, because what it means is, they want to make sure that in case whatever it is turns out to be stupid or fatal, you'll get some of the blame. I mean, if they thought it was any good, they wouldn't want your "input," would they? So you have to somehow escape from the meeting before they get around to asking you anything.

> —*Dave Barry, b. 1947, American humor columnist and author of* Claw Your Way to the Top. *Barry is a Pulitzer Prize–winning syndicated columnist for the* Miami Herald.

—MISTAKES—

To make no mistakes is not in the power of man; but from their errors and mistakes the wise and the good learn wisdom for the future.

> —*Plutarch, fl. first century, Greek biographer best known for* Parallel Lives, *a book that presents character studies of distinguished Greeks and Romans in pairs from the age of Theseus and Romulus to his own day*

When a man has committed no faults in war, he can only have been engaged in it but a short time.

> —*Turenne, 1611–1675, French army field marshal who won fame for his campaigns in the United Provinces during the Dutch War*

Half our mistakes in life arise from feeling where we ought to think, and thinking where we ought to feel.

> —*John Churton Collins, 1848–1908, English author, critic, journalist, professor of English literature at Birmingham, and author of* Voltaire. *Collins is known for his valiant, tenacious effort to gain academic recognition of English in the university curriculum.*

The greatest mistake you can make in life is to be continually fearing you will make one.

> —*Elbert G. Hubbard, 1856–1915, American writer, editor, and painter best known for* A Message to Garcia, *a classical work about taking personal responsibility*

The great mistake is to anticipate the outcome of the engagement; you ought not to be thinking of whether it ends in victory or in defeat. Let nature take its course, and your tools will strike at the right moment.

> —*Bruce Lee, 1940–1973, American martial artist, actor, and co-author of* Tao of Jeet Kune Do. *Born Lee Jun Fan in the Year of the Dragon in San Francisco's Chinatown, Lee created the martial art Jeet Kune Do. Before his death, he was the biggest movie-box-office draw in the world.*

—MONEY—

Money, not purpose, measures the metabolism of corporations. When money runs out and a corporation cannot pay its debts, its creditors take over, and its investors are wiped out, which terrifies all men who save. But no one cares what happens to its employees.

> —*Theodore H. White, 1915–1986, American journalist, author, and historian, from* In Search of History

—MORALS—

It is desirable for a ruler that no man should suffer from cold and hunger under his rule. Man cannot maintain his standard of morals when he has no ordinary means of living.

> —*Kenkò Hoshi, fl. fourteenth century, Japanese Buddhist spiritual leader*

Morality is the custom of one's country and the current feeling of one's peers. Cannibalism is moral in a cannibal country.

—*Samuel Butler, 1612–1680, English satirical poet and author of* Hudibras, *a mock heroic poem satirizing the hypocrisy, churlishness, greed, pride, and casuistry of the Presbyterians and Independents*

I believe the moral losses of expediency always far outweigh the temporary gains.

—*Wendell L. Willkie, 1892–1944, lawyer and Republican nominee for the U.S. presidency in 1940 who toured Egypt, the Middle East, Russia, and China in 1942. He wrote about his experiences and conclusions in* One World.

Wrong is wrong, no matter who does it or who says it.

—*Malcolm X, 1925–1965, American political activist. Malcolm X worked tirelessly as a champion of rights for African Americans.*

Our need to be reminded of the best and the worst in all of us is very strong. That had always been my purpose: to get people back in touch with what makes us so valuable as a human race. We seemed to be drifting as a society—losing touch with the basic concepts of right and wrong.

—*George Lucas, b. 1944, American movie producer, writer, and director. Lucas is the creator of the* Star Wars *and* Indiana Jones *films, which are the most successful movie series of all time. He also founded Industrial Light and Magic, which is considered to be the world's premier special-effects group.*

Using immoral means to achieve a moral purpose is sort of like whoring for virginity. If you use immoral means to achieve a moral end, you become immoral yourself. When you attempt to apply clear black-and-white morality to an issue that is some shade of gray, you are forcing the issue to conform to your personal ideals and presuming to know everything that is necessary to make a sound moral judgment. However, gray-area issues are described as gray because there is no absolute right or wrong about them. Dealing with such issues requires you to simply do what seems best to you, and to have the moral courage to use your best judgment when the answer is unclear.

—Justin K. Roberts, b. 1973, American lawyer. Roberts is a trial lawyer in Salt Lake City, Utah. He was just ten years old when he suggested the protagonist for the book that became Leadership Secrets of Attila the Hun.

—MOTIVATION—

Now, gentlemen, let us do something today which the world may talk of hereafter.

> —*Cuthbert Collingwood, 1748–1810, British navy admiral.*
> *Collingwood used this admonition to*
> *inspire his officers before the Battle of Trafalgar.*

—NEGOTIATION—

Patience may be a virtue, but in negotiating it is a weapon of incalculable power. . . . If you can outwait the other side, you can usually out-negotiate them.

> —*Mark H. McCormack, b. 1930, CEO, International*
> *Management Group. McCormack is the author of*
> On Negotiating *and editor of* The World of Professional Golf.

Use your leverage. The worst thing you can possibly do in a deal is seem desperate to make it. That makes the other guy smell blood, and then you're dead. . . . Leverage is having something the other guy wants. Or better yet, needs. Or best of all, simply can't do without.

> —*Donald J. Trump, b. 1946, American real-estate developer who*
> *is a shrewd businessman known for his flamboyant and*
> *luxurious lifestyle. He is the author of* The Art of the Deal.

—OBEDIENCE—

The leader must himself believe that willing obedience always beats forced obedience, and that he can get this only by really knowing what should be done. Thus he can secure obedience from his men because he can convince them that he knows best, precisely as a good doctor makes patients obey him. Also he must be ready to suffer more hardships than he asks of his soldiers, more fatigue, great extremes of heat and cold.

—Xenophon, c. 431–352 B.C., Greek military leader, historian, and disciple of Socrates. He led ten thousand Greek soldiers in the famous retreat from the battle of Cunaxa.

I have been told that the soldiers will refuse to obey orders in advance. Such a statement leaves me completely unmoved. I know that in all cases where an army has failed to obey its general, this has happened because of some misfortune brought on by the general's incompetence or else because some crime of the general's has been discovered and he has been convicted of avarice.

—Julius Caesar, 100–44 B.C., Roman general, statesman, and dictator, from War Commentaries of Caesar. *Julius Caesar was a patrician by birth. He gained his reputation as a battlefield commander with his victories in Gaul. Caesar was offered but refused the crown. Although he was one of the great military leaders of all time, he ultimately failed to sustain the loyalty of men he should have been able to trust. As a result, Brutus, Cassius, and other members of the Roman senate murdered Caesar on the ides of March.*

—OPINIONS—

New opinions are always suspected, and usually opposed, without any other reason but because they are not already common.

> —*John Locke, 1632–1704, English philosopher, diplomat, physician, secretary to the diplomatic mission to Brandenburg, and an adviser to the British government on coinage. He is known as "the father of English empiricism."*

Opinions founded on prejudice are always sustained with the greatest violence.

> —*Francis Jeffrey, 1773–1850, Scottish co-founder of the* Edinburgh Review, *judge of the Court of Session, member of Parliament, and lord advocate. Jeffrey was highly influential but sometimes inflexible as a critic. He is known for his attacks on romantics.*

True opinion can prevail only if the facts to which they refer are known, if they are not known, false ideas are just as effective as true ones, if not a little more effective.

> —*Walter Lippmann, 1889–1974, American journalist, editor, founder and associate editor of* New Republic, *editor of the* New York World, *and columnist for the* New York Herald Tribune. *He received Pulitzer Prizes in 1958 and 1962 and is the author of* A Preface to Politics.

—OPPORTUNITY—

Carpe diem, quam minimus credula postero. (Seize today, and put as little trust as you can in tomorrow.)

> —*Horace, 65–8 B.C., Roman satirical poet and soldier who commanded a legion in the Republican Army at Philippi and later lived mainly on the patronage of Maecenas*

Some say opportunity knocks only once. That is not true. Opportunity knocks all the time, but you have to be ready for it. If the chance comes, you must have the equipment to take advantage of it.

> —*Louis L'Amour, 1908–1988, American author who wrote under a strict regime of five pages per day every day. As he finished one book, he would start another immediately. He authored over one hundred books, including* How the West Was Won, *and was awarded the U.S. Medal of Freedom in 1984.*

Opportunities are usually disguised as hard work, so most people don't recognize them.

> —*Ann Landers, b. 1918, American columnist. Esther P. Lederer is America's most beloved columnist and writes under the pseudonym Ann Landers.*

—ORGANIZATIONAL DISCIPLINE—

The commander should practice kindness and severity, should appear friendly to the soldiers, speak to them on the march, visit them while they are cooking, ask them if they are well cared for, and alleviate their needs if they have any. Officers without experience in war should be treated kindly. Their good actions should be praised. Small requests should be granted and they should not be treated in an overbearing manner, but severity is maintained about everything regarding duty. The negligent officer is punished; the man who answers back is made to feel your severity by being reprimanded. . . . Pillaging or argumentative soldiers, or those whose obedience is not immediate, should be punished.

—Frederick II, 1712–1786, Prussian king
known as "Frederick the Great"

That quality which I wish to see the officers possess, who are at the head of the troops, is a cool, discriminating judgment when in action, which will enable them to decide with promptitude how far they can go and ought to go, with propriety; and to convey their orders, and act with such vigor and decision, that the soldiers will look up to them with confidence in the moment of action, and obey them with alacrity.

—Arthur Wellesley, 1769–1852, British prime minister and
first duke of Wellington, known as "the Iron Duke." His defeat
of Napoleon at Waterloo ended the Napoleonic Wars.

It is not a matter of one general being better than another, but of one general being better than two.

—David Lloyd George, 1863–1945, British Liberal politician, prime minister, solicitor, secretary of state for war, and author. David Lloyd George directed Britain's policies leading to victory in World War I, instituted negotiations that resulted in the founding of the Irish Free State, and designed Britain's first comprehensive health and unemployment insurance programs.

A soldier who habitually breaks regulations must be dismissed from the army. Vagabonds and vicious people must not be accepted for service. The opium habit must be forbidden, and a soldier who cannot break himself of it should be dismissed.

—Mao Zedong, 1893–1976, Chinese revolutionary and founding leader of the People's Republic of China and supreme leader of China's Communist Party. "Chairman" Mao was also known as Mao Tse-tung.

—ORGANIZATIONAL POLITICS—

It is folly to censure him whom all the world adores.

—Publilius Syrus, fl. first century B.C., Syrian-born Roman writer who arrived in Rome as a slave. He is known for his versified aphorisms.

It is much safer to obey than to rule.

—Thomas à Kempis, c. 1380–1471, German ecclesiastic and writer. An Augustinian monk, Thomas à Kempis is the reputed author of the religious classic De Imitatione Christi *(Imitation of Christ).*

Be wiser than other people, if you can, but do not tell them so.

—Philip Dormer Stanhope, 1694–1773, English fourth earl of Chesterfield, member of Parliament, ambassador to Holland, and lord lieutenant to Ireland. Stanhope's Letters to His Son *provided shrewd, witty, and well-phrased guides to manners, pleasing others, and worldly success.*

It is dangerous to be right in matters on which the established authorities are wrong.

> —*Voltaire, 1694–1778, French satirical writer and wit.*
> *Voltaire is the assumed name of François-Marie Arouet.*
> *His expertise in satire landed him in prison at Bastille,*
> *where he finished his first tragedy,* Oedipe. *He also became*
> *known as a defender of victims of religious intolerance.*

The danger chiefly lies in acting well: No crime's so great as daring to excel.

> —*Charles Churchill, 1731–1764, English satirical*
> *poet who achieved fame with his* Rosciad,
> *which is a fierce attack on actors of the day*

If ever you wish to rise a step above your present degree, you must learn that maxim of the art of war, of currying favor with your superiors; and you must not only cringe to the commander-in-chief himself, but you must take especial care to keep in with his favorites, and dance attendance on his secretary.

> —*Francis Grose, 1731–1791, English antiquary, writer, and*
> *soldier. Grose is the author of* Advice to Officers of the British
> Army *and of* A Classical Dictionary of the Vulgar Tongue,
> *a book that led to the modern-day phrase "That's gross!"*
> *said in reference to something distasteful.*

Private feelings must always be sacrificed for the public service.

> —*Frederick Marryat, 1792–1848, British naval officer*
> *and novelist known as "Captain Marryat"*

Do not engage in any paper wars.

> —*Florence Nightingale, 1820–1910, English nurse and medical*
> *reformer known as "the Lady of the Lamp" for her nightly rounds*

From a worldly point of view there is no mistake so great as that of being always right.

> —*Samuel Butler, 1835–1902, English writer and New Zealand*
> *sheep rancher. Butler was a strong opponent of Darwinism*
> *and satirized family life in Victorian England.*

Long ago I had learned that in conversation with an irate senior, a junior should confine himself to the three remarks, "Yes, sir," "No, sir," and "Sorry, sir." Repeated in the proper sequence, they will get him through the most difficult interview with the minimum discomfort.

> —*William Slim, 1891–1970, British first viscount of Yarralumia*
> *and of Bishopston. Slim led the famous 14th "Forgotten Army"*
> *to victory over the Japanese in Burma during World War II.*

Men in authority will always think that criticism of their policies is dangerous. They will always equate their policies with patriotism, and find criticism subversive.

> —*Henry Steele Commager, 1902–1998, American*
> *educator and author of* The American Mind

No matter how much self-assurance you've demonstrated in a risky situation, particularly a new job, you may look up one day to see the wolves circling. I think that when you're in a new position it's best to do as much one-on-one work as possible and avoid group settings. People are less receptive and enthusiastic in a pack situation, because they're watching everyone else. They also can get mean.

—*Kate White, b. 1950, American editor and author, from* Why Good Girls Don't Get Ahead but Gutsy Girls Do. *White was editor-in-chief of* Working Woman *before becoming editor-in-chief of* Cosmopolitan.

—ORIGINALITY—

Originality consists in thinking for yourself and not in thinking unlike other people.

> —*James Fitzjames Stephen, 1829–1894, English historian and judge, High Court of Justice. Stephen wrote* General View of the Criminal Law of England, *which was the first attempt since Blackstone to explain the principles of English law.*

—OVERCONFIDENCE—

He that is too secure is not safe.

> —*English proverb*

Danger breeds best on too much confidence.

> —*Pierre Corneille, 1606–1684, French dramatist and founder of classical French tragedy*

—PATIENCE—

Our patience will achieve more than our force.

> —*Edmund Burke, 1729–1797, British statesman and political philosopher. Burke was secretary of Ireland and a member of Parliament.*

Good ideas are not adopted automatically. They must be driven into practice with courageous patience.

> —*Hyman G. Rickover, 1900–1986, Russian-born American navy admiral. Rickover directed the planning and construction of the world's first atomic-powered submarine, the U.S.S.* Nautilus. *He was controversial and outspoken and often used unorthodox methods to achieve his goals.*

—PEOPLE SKILLS—

Do not do to others what angers you if done to you by others.

> —*Isocrates, 436–338 B.C., Greek orator, rhetorician, and educator. Isocrates founded a school in Athens where he taught young men of great promise. He was a leader of conservative, Panhellenic opinion.*

Whoever interrupts the conversation of others to make a display of his fund of knowledge makes notorious his own stock of ignorance.

> —*Sa'dī, c. 1213–1291, Persian poet. Sa'dī wrote didactic stories in verse that illustrated Muslim virtues.*

Tempt not a desperate man.

> —*William Shakespeare, 1564–1616, English dramatist and poet. This advice is a line of the character Romeo in Shakespeare's* Romeo and Juliet, *Act V, Scene III. William Shakespeare is the most prominent dramatist in history and prospered financially for his work. His plays continue to be popular today, and Shakespearean festivals are held annually from Stratford-upon-Avon to Cedar City, Utah.*

Punctuality is the politeness of kings.

> —*Louis XVIII, 1755–1824, French royal who served as the titular king of France in exile until the fall of Napoleon in 1814*

More people are flattered into virtue than bullied out of vice.

> —*Robert Smith Surtees, 1803–1864, English journalist, co-founder of* New Sporting Magazine, *and creator of the humorous character Mr. John Jorrocks, a fox-hunting cockney grocer*

Next to ingratitude, the most painful thing to bear is gratitude.

> —*Henry Ward Beecher, 1813–1887, American religious leader and Congregationalist minister. The fiery Beecher defended temperance and denounced slavery.*

The ability to deal with people is as purchasable a commodity as sugar or coffee. And I pay more for that ability than for any other under the sun.

> —*John D. Rockefeller, 1839–1937, founder and CEO, Standard Oil Company. Rockefeller was active in the oil business for his entire career. He established the Rockefeller Institute for Medical Research and the Rockefeller Foundation.*

There are few things that so touch us with instinctive revulsion as a breach of decorum.

> —*Thorstein Veblen, 1857–1929, American economist, social scientist, and author of* The Theory of Business Enterprise

It seldom pays to be rude. It never pays to be only half-rude.

> —*Norman Douglas, 1868–1952, British author, diplomat, and author of* Siren Land

Gratitude is the most exquisite form of courtesy.

> —*Jacques Maritain, 1882–1973, French philosopher, writer, diplomat, and author of* Moral Philosophy

There are two insults which no human will endure: the assertion that he hasn't a sense of humor, and the doubly impertinent assertion that he has never known trouble.

—*Sinclair Lewis, 1885–1951, American novelist, journalist, and editor who was the first American to be awarded a Nobel Prize for Literature (1930). He is the author of* Elmer Gantry.

When dealing with people, let us remember we are not dealing with creatures of logic. We are dealing with creatures of emotion, creatures bustling with prejudices and motivated by pride and vanity.

> —Dale Carnegie, 1888–1955, American motivational
> speaker and author best known for his book
> How to Win Friends and Influence People

Don't paint people into a corner. This makes them dangerous, paranoid, and obstinate.

> —Brian Urquhart, b. 1919, British soldier, author, and
> diplomat who held positions in the United Nations

—PERCEPTION—

Besides learning to see, there is another art to be learned—*not to see* what is not.

> —Maria Mitchell, 1818–1889, American astronomer and professor,
> Vassar College. Mitchell established the orbit of a comet discovered
> in 1847, which resulted in her becoming the first woman elected
> to the American Academy of Arts and Sciences.

It may be said with a degree of assurance that not everything that meets the eye is as it appears.

> —Rod Serling, 1924–1975, American television scriptwriter
> and host. The winner of six Emmys, Serling hosted
> The Twilight Zone and Night Gallery.

—PERFECTION—

To stand still on the summit of perfection is difficult, and in the natural course of things, what cannot go forward slips back.

> —*Marcus Velleius Paterculus, c. 19 B.C.–30 A.D., Roman praetor and historian who wrote a compendium of Roman history down to 29 A.D.*

—PERSEVERANCE—

The barriers are not erected which can say to aspiring talents and industry, "This far and no farther."

> —*Ludwig van Beethoven, 1770–1827, German composer who, despite near-deafness, composed nine symphonies, thirty-two piano sonatas, sixteen string quartets, and the* Mass in D

When I have fully decided that a result is worth getting I go ahead on it and make trial after trial until it comes.

> —*Thomas A. Edison, 1847–1931, American inventor and founder of Edison General Electric Company. Edison was the inventor of the lightbulb and phonograph. He received the first of his more than one thousand patents at the age of twenty-one.*

March on. Do not tarry. To go forward is to move toward perfection. March on, and fear not the thorns, or the sharp stones on life's path.

> —*Kahlil Gibran, 1883–1931, Lebanese-born American writer and artist. Gibran wrote his poems and books in both Arabic and English. His writing is deeply romantic, religious, and mystical in nature. He is the author of* The Prophet.

Don't let the bastards grind you down.

> —*Joseph W. Stilwell, 1883–1946, American army general. Stilwell was theater commander of U.S. forces in China, Burma, and India during World War II and served as chief of staff to Chinese general Chiang Kai-shek. Stilwell was fluent in Chinese and became known as "Vinegar Joe" because of his strong-worded statements.*

A man either lives life as it happens to him, meets it head-on and licks it, or he turns his back on it and starts to wither away.

> —*Gene Roddenberry, 1921–1991, American television producer and scriptwriter best known as the creator of* Star Trek

There are days when it takes all you've got just to keep up with the losers.

> —*Robert Orben, b. 1927, American writer, consultant, lecturer, and author of more than forty humor books. Orben was a comedy writer for Jack Paar, Red Skelton, and Dick Gregory. He was a speechwriter for President Gerald Ford and believes "humor is one of the best forms of communication known to man. It can smooth, heal, and build. If you can put someone at ease, you have a friend."*

Most people give up just when they're about to achieve success. They quit on the one-yard line. They give up at the last minute of the game, one foot from a winning touchdown.

> —*H. Ross Perot, b. 1930, founder and CEO, Electronic Data Systems (EDS) and Perot Systems. When two EDS employees were taken hostage by the Iranian government in 1979, Perot directed a successful rescue mission composed of EDS employees and led by Colonel Arthur "Bull" Simons. Perot's candidacy for the U.S. presidency led to the formation of the Reform Party.*

—PERSONAL CONDUCT—

Let nothing be done in your life which will cause you fear if it becomes known to your neighbor.

> —*Epicurus, 341-270 B.C., Greek philosopher who founded epicureanism, a philosophy emphasizing that pleasure is the only good and the end of all morality but that authentic pleasure is found in a life of simplicity, prudence, honor, and justice*

The worst ruler is one who cannot rule himself.

> —*Marcus Porcius Cato, 234–149 B.C., Roman statesman, orator, and author also known as "Cato the Elder" and "Cato the Censor." He tried to restore by legislation the high morals and simplicity of life characteristic in the early days of the Roman Republic. Cato is the author of* Praecepta, *which is a book of maxims.*

Whenever you are doing a thing, though it can be known but to yourself, ask yourself how you would act were all the world looking at you, and act accordingly.

> —*Thomas Jefferson, 1743–1826, third president of the United States. Known as "the Sage of Monticello," Jefferson was also a lawyer, writer, architect, and plantation owner. He chaired the committee that wrote the Declaration of Independence, and, as president, he prohibited the importation of slaves.*

—PERSONAL EXAMPLE—

It is not wise, or even possible, to divorce private behavior from public leadership—though there are those who have gone to great lengths to suggest that this is the only possible view of "enlightened" individuals. They are wrong. They are deceived. By its very nature, true leadership carries with it the burden of being an example. Is it asking too much of *any* public officer, elected by his or her constituents, to stand tall and be a model before the people—not only in the ordinary aspects of leadership but in his or her behavior? If values aren't established and adhered to at the top, behavior down the ranks is seriously jeopardized and undermined. Indeed, in any organization where such is the case—be it a family, a corporation, a society, or a nation—the values being neglected will in time disappear.

—Gordon B. Hinckley, b. 1910, American religious leader, in Standing for Something. *Hinckley is president of the Church of Jesus Christ of Latter-Day Saints.*

—PERSONAL RESPONSIBILITY—

Hold yourself responsible for a higher standard than anybody else expects of you. Never excuse yourself.

—Henry Ward Beecher, 1813–1887, American clergyman. Beecher was a powerful and convincing speaker of wide influence in his day. In an action that grabbed the national newspaper headlines, he was charged with but later acquitted of adultery.

Man must cease attributing his problems to his environment, and learn again to exercise his will—his personal responsibility.

—*Albert Schweitzer, 1875–1965, French physician, theologian, philosopher, and music scholar. While serving as a missionary physician, Schweitzer established the Lambaréné Hospital in French Equatorial Africa. He received a Nobel Prize in 1952.*

You have the ability to get off your butt and find out what life is about. If you don't, that's your problem, not someone else's.

—Jane Fonda, b. 1937, American actor, author, fitness entrepreneur, and political and social activist, in American Heritage, *July/August 2001. Fonda was bestowed "Miss Army Recruiting" of 1962 but gradually became opposed to the Vietnam War and made an infamous trip to Hanoi in 1972, where she was photographed while seated on a North Vietnamese anti-aircraft gun. She has won two Best Actress Oscars in her film career.*

I don't think of myself as a poor deprived ghetto girl who made good. I think of myself as somebody who from an early age knew I was responsible for myself, and I had to make good.

—Oprah Winfrey, b. 1954, American television talk show host, actor, and author. Because her opinion is so highly valued by her viewing audience, books selected for Oprah's Book Club often become best-sellers.

—PERSPECTIVE—

We see things not as they are, but as we are.

—H. M. Tomlinson, 1873–1958, British journalist and novelist. Henry Major Tomlinson was literary editor for Nation *and the author of* The Sea and the Jungle.

Honor wears different coats to different eyes.

—Barbara Tuchman, 1912–1989, American historian and author. Tuchman was awarded Pulitzer Prizes in 1962 and 1971.

—PLANNING—

We should all be concerned about the future because we will have to spend the rest of our lives there.

> —*C. F. Kettering, 1876–1958, American engineer who developed the electric starter for automobiles. As head of research at General Motors, he discovered tetraethyl lead as an anti-knock agent. He also defined the octane rating of fuels.*

There are only two kinds of plans. Plans that might work and plans that won't work. There's no such thing as the perfect plan. You have to take a plan that might work and make it work.

> —*Wesley K. Clark, b. 1944, American army general, supreme Allied commander of NATO, commander-in-chief of U.S. European Command, and commander-in-chief of U.S. Southern Command, in* Waging Modern War. *Clark is perhaps best known for leading NATO in its first conflict in the operation that rooted Serb troops out of Kosovo.*

—POWER—

Lust for power is the most flagrant of all the passions.

> —*Cornelius Tacitus, c. 56–120, Roman historian, orator, quaestor, praetor, and proconsul of Asia. Tacitus's most noted work is* Historiae, *a history covering reigns from Galba to Domitian.*

Knowledge and human power are synonymous.

> —*Francis Bacon, 1561–1626, British first baron of Verulam and Viscount St. Albans, member of Parliament, solicitor general, attorney general, and lord chancellor. Bacon confessed to bribery and corrupt dealing in chancery suits. He was subsequently banished from Parliament and practicing law. He is known for his concise expressions of practical wisdom and shrewd observations of human behavior.*

Power must never be trusted without a check.

> *—John Adams, 1735–1826, second president of the United States. Adams worked as a lawyer, schoolmaster, and writer. He served as defense counsel for the British soldiers accused of the Boston massacre. Adams was also a member of the committee that drafted the Declaration of Independence.*

In the general course of human nature, a power over a man's subsistence amounts to a power over his will.

> *—Alexander Hamilton, 1755–1804, American Federalist politician and first U.S. secretary of the Treasury. Hamilton established the U.S. Central Banking System. He was killed in a duel with Aaron Burr while Burr was vice president of the United States under Thomas Jefferson.*

Men are strong only so long as they represent a strong idea. They become powerless when they oppose it.

> *—Sigmund Freud, 1856–1939, Austrian psychoanalyst known as "the father of psychoanalysis." Freud saw all human behavior as motivated by drives or instincts, which are in turn the neurological representation of physical needs.*

Power should not be concentrated in the hands of so few, and powerlessness in the hands of so many.

> *—Maggie Kuhn, 1905–1995, American writer and activist who was an advocate for women and the elderly and founded the Gray Panthers*

The power to do good is also the power to do harm; those who control the power today may not tomorrow; and, more important, what one man regards as good, another may regard as harm.

—*Milton Friedman, b. 1912, American economist, author, professor at the University of Chicago, and senior research fellow at the Hoover Institution. Friedman is an advocate of limited government and free enterprise. He received a Nobel Prize in 1976.*

You only have power over people so long as you don't take *everything* away from them. But when you've robbed a man of everything he's no longer in your power—he's free again.

—*Aleksander Solzhenitsyn, b. 1918, Russian novelist who spent eight years in a labor camp for criticizing Stalin. He was exiled from Russia in 1974 but allowed to return in 1994. Solzhenitsyn is the author of* One Day in the Life of Ivan Denisovich. *He was awarded a Nobel Prize in 1970.*

—PREJUDICE—

There is nothing men more readily give themselves to than pushing their own beliefs. When ordinary means fail, they add commandment, violence, fire, and sword.

—*Michel Eyquem de Montaigne, 1533–1592, French philosopher, essayist, counselor of the Parliament of Bordeaux, and mayor of Bordeaux. Montaigne's fame stems from his book* Essais, *which reflects his spirit of skepticism and had a major influence on French and English literature.*

We must remember that we have to make judges out of men, and that by being made judges their prejudices are not diminished and their intelligence is not increased.

—*Robert G. Ingersoll, 1833–1899, American lawyer, orator, and promoter of secular religion known as agnosticism*

Everyone is a prisoner of his own experiences. No one can eliminate prejudices—just recognize them.

—*Edward R. Murrow, 1908–1965, American journalist and radio and television producer. Murrow became famous for his broadcasts from London during the blitz. He produced and narrated the* Hear It Now *radio show and produced and hosted the* See It Now *television program. Murrow also served as head of the U.S. Information Agency.*

Nothing in the world is more dangerous than a sincere ignorance and conscientious stupidity.

> —*Martin Luther King Jr., 1929–1968, American Baptist minister and civil rights leader. King opposed discrimination by organizing nonviolent resistance and peaceful mass demonstrations. He literally gave his life fighting for the cause of civil rights by way of his assassination. He was awarded a Nobel Prize in 1964. King's birthday, January 15, is a legal holiday in the United States.*

—PREPARATION—

Where observation is concerned, chance favors only the prepared mind.

> —*Louis Pasteur, 1822–1895, French chemist and bacteriologist. Pasteur was a pioneer in vaccination techniques and devised pasteurization—a partial sterilization process that destroys objectionable organisms in perishable food products without altering the substance.*

The stroke of genius that turns the fate of a battle? I don't believe in it. A battle is a complicated operation that you prepare laboriously. If the enemy does this, you say to yourself I will do that. If such and such happens, these are the steps I shall take to meet it. You think out every possible development and decide on the way to deal with the situation created. One of these developments occurs; you put your plan in operation, and everyone says, "What genius . . ." whereas the credit is really due to the labor of preparation.

> —*Ferdinand Foch, 1851–1929, French army general and senior French representative at the World War I armistice negotiations*

—PRIDE—

Pride goeth before destruction, and an haughty spirit before a fall.

—Proverbs 16:18, The King James Bible

Don't be proud of dumb things. It's dumb to be proud of production records rather than products. It's dumb to be proud of a plant rather than the working conditions of your employees. It's dumb to flaunt your wealth and then try to tell employees that times are tough, vacations must be canceled, etc. It's dumb to ask employees to make sacrifices you are not willing to make in kind.

—Lois Wyse, b. 1926, president, Wyse Advertising Inc.
Wyse is the author of some sixty books.

—PROBLEM SOLVING—

Divide each difficulty into as many parts as is feasible and necessary to resolve it.

—René Descartes, 1596–1650, French philosopher and
mathematician. In his famed treatise, Discours de la méthode, *he*
attempted to unify all knowledge as the product of clear reasoning
from self-evident premises. He also developed the dualistic theory
of mind and matter as separate though interacting.

Sometimes a fool makes a good suggestion.

—Nicolas Boileau-Despréaux, 1636–1711, French critic, poet, and
author of L'Art poétique, *which is considered to be a definitive*
statement of the principles of classic French verse

To solve a problem it is necessary to think. It is necessary to think even to decide what facts to collect.

> —*Robert Maynard Hutchins, 1899–1977, author, dean of Yale Law School, and chancellor of the University of Chicago. As chancellor of the University of Chicago, Hutchins introduced a "Great Books" undergraduate program and abolished intercollegiate football. He is the author of* The Higher Learning in America.

Bromidic though it may sound, some questions don't have answers, which is a terribly difficult lesson to learn.

> —*Katharine Graham, 1917-2001, American journalist; chairman, executive committee, the Washington Post Company; chairman, CEO, and president, the Washington Post Company; publisher, the* Washington Post. *Graham served as chairman and president of the American Newspaper Publishers Association and was a board member of the National Campaign to Reduce Teenage Pregnancy.*

It may sound strange, but I also invite confrontation. Confrontation leads to truth. People know better than to agree with what I say simply because I say it. I don't want that. I don't respect it. I like issues to be thoroughly debated to take advantage of the best our minds have to offer. If there's a problem, it is a company problem that will be solved by the management team.

> —*Sumner Redstone, b. 1923, American lawyer, chairman and CEO of Viacom, and law professor at the University of San Francisco and Boston College, from* A Passion to Win. *Born in a Boston tenement, Redstone served in a U.S. army cryptography unit whose assignment was to crack Japanese code during World War II.*

The only people who have the easy answers are the people who don't have the responsibility.

—*Clarence J. Thomas, b. 1948, U.S. Supreme Court justice.*
Thomas was the first "baby boomer" to be appointed to the Supreme
Court. He is justice number 106 in the history of the Court.

—PROBLEMS—

May you have a brilliant idea, which you know is right, and be unable to convince others.

—*Romanian curse*

Entities must not be multiplied beyond what is necessary.

—*William of Occam, 1285–1349, English philosopher and theologian.*
Occam based scientific knowledge on experience, self-evident truths,
and logical propositions resulting from those two sources. The foregoing
observation is known as Occam's razor, which is expressed often as "A
problem should be stated in its basic and simplest terms." There are
other forms given to Occam's razor, the most colloquial being the
acronym K.I.S.S., which stands for "Keep it simple, stupid!"

The difficulties you meet will resolve themselves as you advance. Proceed, and light will dawn, and shine with increasing clearness on your path.

—*Jean Le Rond d'Alembert, 1717–1783, French mathematician,*
philosopher, and physicist who was raised in a foster family.
D'Alembert's book Réflexions sur la cause générale des vents
contains his discovery of partial differential equations and explains
the precession of equinoxes and the rotation of the Earth's axis.

"Difficulties" is the name given to things which it is our business to overcome.

> —*Ernest J. King, 1878–1956, American navy admiral and chief of naval operations. King served as commander in chief of the combined Atlantic fleet during World War II.*

Problems are only opportunities in work clothes.

> —*Henry J. Kaiser, 1882–1967, American industrialist. Kaiser's companies were involved in dam construction, shipbuilding, steel production, and automobile manufacturing. He is the founder of the Kaiser Foundation for Health Services.*

Never underestimate a problem or your ability to cope with it. Realize that the problem you are facing has been faced by millions of human beings. You have untapped potential for dealing with a problem if you will take the problem and your own undeveloped, unchanneled powers seriously. Your reaction to a problem as much as the problem itself will determine the outcome. I have seen people face the most catastrophic problems with a positive mental attitude, turning their problems into creative experience. They turned their scars into stars.

> —*Robert H. Schuller, b. 1926, founder, Garden Grove Community Church and the Hour of Power television ministry. Schuller is the author of* Tough Times Don't Last, but Tough People Do.

The grave worries facing the world today mostly don't have solutions. That is, they don't have solutions outside ourselves. We can't vote our troubles away. Or mail them to Washington either. We can't give fifty dollars to the Sierra Club, read Douglas Coupland, and sing the *Captain Planet* theme song and set everything right. Instead we have to accept the undramatic and often extremely boring duties of working hard, exercising self-control, taking care of ourselves, our families, and our neighbors, being kind, and practicing as much private morality as we can stand without popping.

—P. J. O'Rourke, b. 1947, American journalist, editor, and author, from All the Trouble in the World. *O'Rourke began his career writing and editing an underground "anti-war," "anti-capitalist" newspaper in Baltimore. He was editor in chief of* National Lampoon *and now writes for* Rolling Stone. *The* London Times *calls him "the gunslinger of the eminently respectable school of American right-wing libertarian philosophers."*

—PROFITS—

Profit is today a fighting word. Profits are the lifeblood of the economic system, the magic elixir upon which progress and all good things depend ultimately. But one man's lifeblood is another man's cancer.

> —*Paul A. Samuelson, b. 1915, American economist.*
> *Samuelson held many international advisory positions,*
> *including a seat on the Federal Reserve Board. His book,*
> Foundations of Economic Analysis, *helped revive neo-classical*
> *economics. He was awarded a Nobel Prize in 1970.*

—PROGRESS—

The greater part of progress is the desire to progress.

> —*Seneca, c. 4 B.C.–65 A.D., Roman moralist, Stoic philosopher,*
> *and politician. Called "Seneca the Younger," he began his*
> *political career as a quaestor. He was banished to Corsica for*
> *alleged adultery with the emperor's niece and later was*
> *recalled to tutor Domitius, who became emperor under the*
> *name Nero. Seneca was later accused of complicity in*
> *conspiracy with Pisó and ordered by Nero to kill himself.*

The only way to discover the limits of the possible is to go beyond them into the impossible.

> —*Arthur C. Clarke, b. 1917, English science-fiction*
> *writer best known for* 2001: A Space Odyssey

—PUBLIC OPINION—

It is a folly of too many to mistake the echo of a London coffeehouse for the voice of the kingdom.

—*Jonathan Swift, 1667–1745, Irish satirist, poet, author, and Anglican cleric best known for his book* Gulliver's Travels

Private opinion is weak, but public opinion is almost omnipotent.

—*Harriet Beecher Stowe, 1811–1896, American novelist, humanitarian, and author of* Uncle Tom's Cabin, *a book that strengthened the abolitionist movement with its description of the sufferings caused by slavery*

—PUNISHMENT—

The object of punishment is prevention from evil; it can never be made impulsive to the good.

—*Horace Mann, 1796–1859, American educator and politician considered to be the father of American public education*

—RAPPORT—

The commander must try, above all, to establish personal and comradely contact with his men, but without giving away an inch of his authority.

—*Erwin Rommel, 1891–1944, German army field marshal. Called "the Desert Fox," Rommel was one of the twentieth century's great battlefield commanders. He was forced to commit suicide over his opposition to Hitler.*

—RECIPROCITY—

If you believe in me, I'll believe in you.

—Lewis Carroll, 1832–1898, English author. Lewis Carroll is the pseudonym of Charles Lutwidge Dodgson. He is the author of Alice's Adventures in Wonderland.

I believe that you can get everything in life you want if you will just help enough other people get what they want.

—Zig Ziglar, b. 1926, American inspirational writer and speaker. Ziglar is one of twelve children born to his parents, and he began his career in sales. His first best-seller was See You at the Top. *Today, Zig Ziglar is regarded by many as "the king of motivational speakers."*

—RECOGNITION—

Even if strength fails, boldness at least will deserve praise: in great endeavors even to have had the will is enough.

—Sextus Propertius, c. 50–15 B.C., Roman elegiac poet. Propertius left his home in Umbria to live in Rome, where he became closely associated with Ovid and Virgil. His poems were mostly expressions of sexual love and were first dedicated to his mistress, Hostia.

Nothing so soon the drooping spirits can raise as praises from the men whom all men praise.

—Abraham Cowley, 1618–1667, English poet. Cowley is the author of The Mistress *and was heavily involved with botany and experimental science. He is buried in Westminster Abby.*

As to rewards and promotion, it is essential to respect long service and at the same time open a way for merit.

—*Jomini, 1779–1869, French baron, army general, and writer. Jomini joined the Russian army and served as aide-de-camp to Alexander I and Nicholas I.*

The credit belongs to the man who is actually in the arena; whose face is marred by dust and sweat and blood; who strives valiantly; who errs and comes up short again and again; who knows the great enthusiasms, the great devotions, and spends himself in a worthy cause; who at the best knows in the end triumph of high achievement; and who at the worst, if he fails, at least he fails while daring greatly.

—Theodore Roosevelt, 1858–1919, twenty-sixth president of the United States. During the Spanish-American War, "Teddy" Roosevelt organized and commanded a volunteer cavalry known as "the Rough Riders."

Nothing else can quite substitute for a few well-chosen, well-timed, sincere words of praise. They're absolutely free— and worth a fortune.

—Sam Walton, 1918–1992, founder and CEO, Wal-Mart Inc. Walton began his career in retail at J. C. Penney. Before starting Wal-Mart, Walton founded Ben Franklin and Walton's 5 & 10 stores. Walton is a legend in self-service retailing and was a great motivator as a leader.

—REPUTATION—

Of the best rulers, the people know they exist; the next best they love and praise; the next they fear; and the next they revile.

—Lao-tzu, fl. 565 B.C., Chinese philosopher and founder of taoism

Associate yourself with men of good quality if you esteem your own reputation; for 'tis better to be alone than in bad company.

—George Washington, 1732–1799, general, plantation owner,
and first president of the United States. Washington was
commander in chief of the army of the colonies during the
Revolutionary War. He is known as "the father of his country."

The great difficulty is first to win a reputation; the next to keep it while you live; and the next to preserve it after you die.

—Benjamin Haydon, 1786–1846, English artist. Haydon
is known for his historical and biblical paintings, which
include Judgment of Solomon *and* Raising of Lazarus.

—RESILIENCE—

You may have a fresh start any moment you choose, for this thing that we call "failure" is not the falling down, but the staying down.

> —*Mary Pickford, 1893–1979, Canadian-born American actor. A co-founder of United Artists, Pickford was a star of silent movies and received an Academy Award in 1927.*

In the final analysis, the question of why bad things happen to good people transmits itself into some very different questions, no longer asking why something happened, but asking how we will respond, what we intend to do now that it has happened.

> —*Harold S. Kushner, b. 1935, American Jewish rabbi and author, from* When Bad Things Happen to Good People

—RESPECT—

Give the laborer his wage before his perspiration be dry.

> —*Muhammad, c. 570–632, Arabian religious leader and founder of Islam. Muhammad experienced a vision c. 610, in which he received a prophetic call. After this, he had periodic revelations that he held to be from God (Allah), 650 of which were written down as the Koran, the sacred scripture of Islam.*

Always recognize that human individuals are ends, and do not use them as a means to your ends.

> —*Immanuel Kant, 1724–1804, German philosopher and educator. Kant attempted to determine the nature and limits of human knowledge, the necessary categories of consciousness, and their ethical and aesthetic consequences. He had a major conflict with the Prussian government as the result of his liberal religious views. He is the author of* Critique of Practical Reason *and* Critique of Judgment.

Trust men, and they will be true to you; treat them greatly, and they will show themselves great.

—*Ralph Waldo Emerson, 1803–1882,*
American philosopher and poet.
Emerson became associated with
German idealism and evolved the
concept of transcendentalism,
which found expression in
his essay Nature.

Nothing should be made by man's labor which is not worth making, or which must be made by labor degrading to the makers.

—*William Morris, 1834–1896, English artist, writer, and printer*

If anyone is to remain pleased with you, he should be pleased with himself whenever he thinks of you.

—*Francis Herbert Bradley, 1846–1924, Welsh philosopher and writer. Despite being a semi-invalid for most of his life, Bradley was the most influential figure in the British idealist movement of the time. His most notable work was* Appearance and Reality.

Any use of a human being, in which less is demanded of him and less is attributed to him than his full status, is degradation and a waste.

—*Norbert Wiener, 1894–1964, American scientist best known for establishing the science of cybernetics, which earned him the title "father of automation"*

In real life, the most practical advice for leaders is not to treat pawns as pawns, nor princes like princes, but all persons like persons.

—*James MacGregor Burns, b. 1918, American political scientist, author, professor at Williams College, and senior scholar at the James MacGregor Burns Leadership Academy at the University of Maryland. Burns served as a member of the Hoover Commission. He is a proponent of leadership that holds the best interests of the governed high above political gain. Burns won a Pulitzer Prize in 1970.*

—RESPONSIBILITY—

However tempting it might be to some, when much trouble lies ahead, to step aside adroitly and put someone else up to take the blows, I do not intend to take that cowardly course, but, on the contrary, to stand up to my post and persevere according to my duty as I see it.

> —*Winston Churchill, 1874–1965, British prime minister, home secretary, first lord of the Admiralty, chancellor of exchequer, and member of Parliament. Churchill is one of the greatest statesmen in history and certainly one of the most colorful. He is author of* History of the English-Speaking Peoples *and was awarded a Nobel Prize in 1953.*

Genuine responsibility exists only where there is real responding.

> —*Martin Buber, 1878–1965, Austrian-born Israeli religious philosopher. Buber was editor of the Zionist weekly* Die Welt, *founded and edited* Der Jude, *and was a professor at Hebrew University. He also made a German translation of the Hebrew Bible.*

There are two kinds of people: those who do the work and those who take the credit. Try to be in the first group; there is less competition there.

> —*Indira Gandhi, 1917–1984, prime minister of India. A well-cultured woman with an authoritarian streak, Gandhi was a tough and shrewd politician. Although she acquired a formidable international reputation as a "statesman," Gandhi used the military to resolve internal disputes and encouraged a culture of sycophancy and nepotism within the Indian government.*

—RISK TAKING—

He who risks nothing gets nothing.

—French proverb

He that leaveth nothing to chance will do few things ill, but he will do very few things.

—George Savile, 1633–1695, British essayist, president of Privy Council, lord privy seal and chief minister of the crown, and marquis of Halifax. Savile was one of the first political pamphleteers.

Success tends to go not to the person who is error-free, because he also tends to be risk-averse. Rather it goes to the person who recognizes that life is pretty much a percentage business. It isn't making mistakes that's critical; it's correcting them and getting on with the principal task.

—Donald H. Rumsfeld, b. 1932, congressman, ambassador to NATO, White House chief of staff, twice-appointed U.S. secretary of defense, CEO and chairman of G. D. Searle & Company, and CEO and chairman of General Instrument Corporation. Rumsfeld is best known for being the youngest defense secretary in history. As White House chief of staff, he distributed a manual, "Rumsfeld's Rules," to the staff, rule number one being: "Don't play president—you're not."

You've got to be able to step off the dock. You've got to be able to take chances and risks if you're ever going to make anything of yourself. If you don't, you'll be just like everybody else.

—William Castle DeVries, b. 1943, American surgeon. DeVries was the first surgeon in the world to implant an artificial heart in a human. After being diagnosed with arrhythmia, DeVries retired from surgery at age fifty-five.

Don't screw up! Real leaders often make unpopular decisions and take calculated risks in situations where the eventual outcome is not clear because it's the right thing to do. Make decisions based on anything else and you're screwing up.

—*J. D. Brisk, b. 1959, co-founder and CEO, Keylabs Inc. Keylabs is information technology's largest independent test lab and a pioneer in network testing.*

—RULES—

No rule is so general which admits no exception.

> —*Robert Burton, 1577–1640, English writer. Burton's great work was* Anatomy of Melancholy, *a learned miscellany of the ideas of his time.*

—SALESMANSHIP—

The definition of salesmanship is the gentle art of letting the customer have it your way.

> —*Ray Kroc, 1902–1984, founder of McDonald's Corporation and salesman. When fifteen years old, Kroc lied about his age in order to become an ambulance driver for the Red Cross. In 1954, Kroc made a deal with the McDonald brothers to sell franchises in their small chain of hamburger stands for $950 each, with 1.4 percent of sales payable to him and 0.5 percent to the McDonald brothers, whom he bought out in 1961 for $2.7 million.*

—SCRUTINY—

Skeptical scrutiny is the means, in both science and religion, by which deep thoughts can be winnowed from deep nonsense.

> —*Carl Sagan, 1934–1996, American astronomer. Sagan demonstrated that amino acids can be synthesized in an artificial primordial soup irradiated by ultraviolet light—a possible origin of life on earth. He is the author of* Cosmos.

—SELF-AWARENESS—

In other living creatures the ignorance of themselves is nature, but in men it is vice.

> —*Boethius, 480–524, Roman counsel and philosopher. A close adviser to Theodoric, the Ostrogoth ruler of Rome, for a time, Boethius was later accused of conspiracy against him, which led to Boethius's execution without a trial.*

The greatest of faults, I should say, is to be conscious of none.

> —*Thomas Carlyle, 1795–1881, Scottish historian, political philosopher, and author. German romanticism influenced Carlyle's writing. His book* History of the French Revolution *celebrates the force of the "strong, just man" against the degraded masses.*

What is necessary to change a person is to change his awareness of himself.

> —*Abraham H. Maslow, 1908–1970, American psychologist and founder of humanistic psychology who introduced the concept of the human-needs hierarchy*

Never believe your press clippings. It is easy for leaders to get too full of themselves. That's wrong. Remember who you are and be true to yourself and you'll be fine.

> —*Robert S. Coffey, b. 1943, American army lieutenant general. Coffey was the last commanding general of the fabled 2nd Armored "Hell on Wheels" Division before its colors were retired at Fort Hood, Texas, as part of the American military's downsizing following the end of the Cold War. He later served as the deputy commanding general of the U.S. Army in Europe.*

—SELF-CONCEPT—

Public opinion is a weak tyrant compared with our own private opinion. What a man thinks of himself, that is which determines, or rather indicates, his fate.

> —*Henry David Thoreau, 1817–1862, American essayist and poet. Thoreau was a prominent figure of transcendentalism. His book* On the Duty of Civil Disobedience *was a major influence on Mahatma Gandhi's policy of passive resistance.*

No man can make you feel inferior without your consent.

> —*Eleanor Roosevelt, 1884–1962, American first lady. Eleanor Roosevelt was married to President Franklin D. Roosevelt. She was involved with a number of liberal causes and became chair of the U.N. Commission on Human Rights.*

—SELF-CONTROL—

Remember that there is always a limit to self-indulgence, but none to self-restraint.

> —*Mahatma Gandhi, 1869–1948, Indian nationalist and spiritual leader. Gandhi was the most prominent opponent of British rule of India. He is best remembered for his non-violent policy of passive resistance.*

—SELF-IMPROVEMENT—

Happiness is neither virtue nor pleasure nor this thing nor that but simply growth. We are happy when we are growing.

—William Butler Yeats, 1865–1939, Irish poet and dramatist. Yeats's play The Countess Cathleen *and collection of stories* The Celtic Twilight *helped stimulate Ireland's literary revival. He received a Nobel Prize in 1923.*

—SELFISHNESS—

The same people who can deny others everything are famous for refusing themselves nothing.

—Leigh Hunt, 1784–1859, British essayist, poet, editor of The Examiner *and* The Reflector, *and founder and editor of* The Indicator. *Hunt was imprisoned for two years for giving bad press to the Prince Regent.*

When a man is wrapped up in himself he makes a pretty small package.

—John Ruskin, 1819–1900, English art and social critic. Ruskin took on Renaissance art in The Stone of Venice *and lashed out at capitalism in* The Political Economy of Art.

—SELFLESSNESS—

The highest of distinctions is service to others.

—George VI, 1895–1952, British noble who became king of Great Britain on the abdication of his brother Edward VIII

—SELF-PITY—

Let not your mind run on what you lack as much as on what you have already.

—Marcus Aurelius, 121–180, Roman emperor and Stoic philosopher. Aurelius was occupied for most of his reign in fighting off Germanic tribes. He is best remembered for Meditations, *a collection of aphorisms and reflections.*

—SITUATIONAL LEADERSHIP—

Fit no stereotypes. Don't chase the latest management fad. The situation dictates which approach best accomplishes the team's mission.

—Daniel "Chappie" James, 1920–1978, American air force general. James was one of the famed Tuskegee Airmen, the first African American pilots in the U.S. Army Air Corps. Noted for his patriotism and sterling character, James later became the first African American promoted to the rank of general.

—SKEPTICISM—

Skepticism is the chastity of the intellect, and it is shameful to surrender it too soon or to the first comer: There is nobility in preserving it coolly and proudly through a long youth, until at last, in the ripeness of instinct and discretion, it can be safely exchanged for fidelity and happiness.

—George Santayana, 1863–1952, Spanish-born American philosopher and writer. Santayana is the author of Realms of Being, *a book of poetry, and* The Last Puritan, *a novel.*

—SLANDER—

Slander is worse than cannibalism.

—John Chrysostom, c. 347–407, Syrian prelate. Chrysostom lived as a hermit monk for a while before he became the archbishop of Constantinople. His eloquent criticisms of the wealthy and powerful caused Empress Eudoxia to banish him, but he was later recalled by popular demand. Known as "Doctor of the Church," he wrote homilies and commentaries that had significant influence in the day, and he was canonized as a saint.

—SOCIAL LIFE—

The most exhausting thing in life is being insincere. That is why so much social life is exhausting.

—Anne Morrow Lindbergh, 1906–2001, American writer. Anne Lindbergh is best known for her five volumes of diaries and letters, which provide a record of her life during the turbulent period of the celebrity of her husband, famed aviator Charles Lindbergh. She was the first woman in the United States to earn a glider pilot's license.

—SOCIAL RESPONSIBILITY—

Great accumulations of property should go back to the community and common purposes.

> —*Alfred Nobel, 1833–1896, Swedish munitions inventor and manufacturer and philanthropist. Nobel invented dynamite, gelignite, and other high explosives. It was the generous endowment from his will that established the annual Nobel Prizes awarded for the encouragement of people who work for the interests of humanity.*

Greed is still around, but it has been tempered by a new reality, that corporate survival is linked in part to a company's attention to its responsible role in society. Part of the new reality is a growing understanding that a healthy environment is a vital link to the bottom line.

> —*Joel Makower, b. 1952, American freelance journalist and author, from* The E Factor

—STAFFING—

Those who labor with their minds govern others; those who labor with their strength are governed by others.

> —*Mencius, c. 372–289 B.C., Chinese philosopher also known as "Meng-tzu"*

The question "Who ought to be boss?" is like asking "Who ought to be the tenor in a quartet?" Obviously, the man who can sing tenor.

> —*Henry Ford, 1863–1947, organizer and president, Ford Motor Company Inc. Ford was a pioneer in employing the assembly-line method for automobile production.*

I divide officers into four classes—the clever, the lazy, the stupid, and the industrious. Each officer possesses at least two of these qualities. Those who are clever and industrious are fitted for the high staff appointments. Use can be made of those who are stupid and lazy. The man who is clever and lazy is fit for the very highest command. He has the temperament and the requisite nerves to deal with all situations. But whoever is stupid and industrious must be removed immediately.

—Baron Kurt von Hammerstein-Equord, 1878–1943,
German army colonel general, chief of the army staff, and
supreme commander of the western front. Von
Hammerstein opposed Hitler and plotted to capture him
when he visited the western front early in World War II but
was relieved from command before he could enact his plan.

Under every system of economy men who can manage men manage men who can only manage things.

—Will Durant, 1885–1981, American historian and author,
from The Story of Civilization, Volume 4, The Age of Faith.
One of the greatest historians ever to have lived, Durant wrote
the classic eleven-volume Story of Civilization *series with his*
wife, Ariel, and it was published over a forty-year period. He
was awarded the Presidential Medal of Freedom in 1977.

Never hire your client's children.

—David Ogilvy, 1911–1999, English-born founder and CEO, Ogilvy & Mather. Ogilvy was an advertising legend and a respected leader in the advertising industry for decades. He was the creator of some of the most memorable advertising in the world, including "Commander Schweppes." Ogilvy was made a commander of the British Empire in 1967 and awarded France's Order of Arts and Letters in 1990.

—STEREOTYPING—

What is repugnant to every human being is to be reckoned as a member of a class and not as an individual person.

> —*Dorothy L. Sayers, 1893–1957, English novelist, dramatist, and essayist. Sayers was a celebrated writer of detective stories and gained a reputation as a Christian apologist.*

I am not going to limit myself just because people won't accept the fact that I can do something else.

> —*Dolly Parton, b. 1946, American country-music singer and writer, actor, and creator of the Dollywood theme park in Tennessee*

—STRATEGY—

I believe that you have to understand the economics of a business before you have a strategy, and you have to understand your strategy before you have a structure. If you get these in the wrong order, you will probably fail.

> —*Michael Dell, b. 1965, founder and CEO, Dell Computers Inc., from the keynote address at the Society of American Business Editors and Writers Technology Conference, Dallas, Texas, September 10, 1998. Dell began his career in business by buying old computers and upgrading them for resale. Today, Dell Computers is the largest direct-sales computer manufacturer in the world.*

—SUCCESS—

There are only two ways of getting on in this world; by one's own industry, or by the weakness of others.

> —*Jean de La Bruyère, 1645–1696, French moralist and author. La Bruyère was the grandson of Louis Condé II, the fourth prince de Condé, also known as "the Great Condé." He was also tutor to Louis de Bourbon.*

Let this be understood, then, at starting; that the patient conquest of difficulties which rise in the regular and legitimate channels of business and enterprise is not only essential in securing the success which you seek but it is essential to that preparation of your mind, requisite for the enjoyment of your successes, and for retaining them when gained. . . . So, day by day, and week by week; so, month after month, and year after year, work on, and in that process gain strength and symmetry, and nerve and knowledge, that when success, patiently and bravely worked for, shall come, it may find you prepared to receive it and keep it.

> —*Josiah Gilbert Holland, 1819–1881, American writer and editor of* Scribner's Monthly and Century Magazine. *Holland is the author of* Lessons in Life.

The toughest thing about success is that you've got to keep on being a success.

> —*Irving Berlin, 1888–1989, Russian-born American composer, musical playwright, and song writer. Berlin wrote more than nine hundred songs, including "God Bless America," "Easter Parade," and "White Christmas."*

You've got to like your work. You've got to like what you are doing; you've got to be doing something worthwhile so you can like it—because if it's worthwhile, that makes a difference, don't you see?

> —*Harland Sanders, 1890–1980, founder, Kentucky Fried Chicken. Known as Colonel Sanders, Sanders started the first Kentucky Fried Chicken franchise in Salt Lake City, Utah.*

Sometimes it's worse to win a fight than to lose.

> —*Billie Holiday, 1915–1959, American jazz singer. Born Eleanora Fagan, Holiday began her career with Benny Goodman's band. Her autobiography,* Lady Sings the Blues, *was made into a film.*

Success is the progressive realization of a worthy goal.

> —*Earl Nightingale, 1921–1989, American self-development audiotape pioneer, radio announcer, inspirational speaker, and co-founder of Nightingale-Conant Corporation. Nightingale was the voice of the* Our Changing World *radio program.*

No one that ever lived has ever had enough power, prestige, or knowledge to overcome the basic condition of all life—you win some and you lose some.

> —*Ken Keyes Jr., 1921–1995, American author, personal growth leader, peace advocate, and real-estate agent. Best known for his personal-growth workshops and as the author of* Handbook to Higher Consciousness *and* The Hundredth Monkey, *Keyes contracted polio in 1946 and spent the remainder of his years in a wheelchair as a quadriplegic.*

Never lose sight of the fact that the most important yardstick of your success will be how you treat other people—your family, friends, and coworkers, and even strangers along the way.

—Barbara Bush, b. 1925, American first lady. Barbara Bush is married to former president George H. Bush and mother of President George W. Bush.

Your chances of success are directly proportional to the degree of pleasure you derive from what you do. If you are in a job you hate, face the fact squarely and get out.

—Michael Korda, b. 1933, English-born American author and editor in chief at Simon & Schuster. Korda is famous for his zealous salesmanship and charismatic personality. He edited several volumes of Will and Ariel Durant's masterpiece, The Story of Civilization, *and has authored a number of books himself, including* Power!

Hard work always pays off.

—Stephanie Lynn "Stevie" Nicks, b. 1948, American composer and rock vocalist. Nicks began performing at the age of four. She gained fame as a member of Fleetwood Mac and was inducted into the Rock and Roll Hall of Fame in 1998.

—SYCOPHANTS—

He who praises you for what you lack wishes to take from you what you have.

—Juan Manuel, 1282–1349, Spanish royal, general, and author. Manuel was a prince and general in chief of the Spanish army. Known as Don Juan Manuel, Manuel wrote prose tales in an Oriental manner and was deeply involved in political intrigues of the day.

—TEAM BUILDING—

Superiority of material strength is given to a commander gratis. Superior knowledge and superior tactical skill he must himself acquire. Superior morale, superior cooperation, he must himself create.

> —*Joseph Mason Reeves, 1872–1948, American navy admiral. Reeves was the first naval aviator to be commander in chief of the U.S. fleet and was a member of the commission that investigated the Japanese attack on Pearl Harbor.*

If you have some respect for people as they are, you can be more effective in helping them to become better than they are.

> —*John W. Gardner, b. 1912, American educator, executive, author, U.S. secretary for health, education, and welfare, founder of Common Cause, and president of the Carnegie Foundation for the Advancement of Teaching. Gardner is the author of* Excellence: Can We Be Equal and Excellent Too?

Good leaders in various commands and in lessor positions of authority are not common. Often, they are uncomfortable, have their finger on their number, and are guided by a philosophy of "For God's sake don't let anything untoward happen on my watch." True leaders have a strong identification with the mission, projects, and job at hand. They are true believers full of enthusiasm coupled with honest concern for and with people and their families, and, to the extent possible, are familiar with their people's personal histories. Tell people what is to be done and why. Invite limited discussion. Identify the group as a team. Keep all informed. Be quick to publicly praise worthy performance, and do most of necessary personal criticism in private.

—Lloyd Mark "Pete" Bucher, b. 1927, American navy commander and artist. Bucher was captain of the U.S.S. Pueblo, *an unarmed electronic surveillance ship assigned to operate in the Western Pacific. The ship was illegally seized by naval and air forces of North Korea in January 1968. One man was killed and fourteen wounded during the attack on the ship. The North Koreans held the* Pueblo's *crew in captivity for eleven months. Contrary to reports at the time, Bucher did not surrender. The American flag was still flying when the North Koreans took the* Pueblo *by force. Since his retirement, Bucher has painted more than 350 watercolors of diverse subjects.*

Give your workers more sophisticated jobs along with better tools, and you'll discover that your employees will become more responsible and bring more intelligence to their work. In the digital age you need to make knowledge workers out of every employee possible.

—William Henry "Bill" Gates III, b. 1955, American computer software executive, author, and philanthropist, from Business @ the Speed of Thought. *Gates co-founded Microsoft Corporation with Paul Allen. He is one of the most influential figures of the digital age.*

—TEAMWORK—

One chops the wood; the other does the grunting.

> —*Yiddish proverb*

—TEMPTATION—

It is not the great temptations that ruin us; it is the little ones.

> —*John W. De Forest, 1826–1906, American writer.*
> *De Forest's writing employed striking realism.*
> *He is the author of* Miss Ravenel's Conversion.

—TIME MANAGEMENT—

Time is the most valuable thing a man can spend.

> —*Diogenes, fl. third century* A.D., *Greek writer who authored*
> Peri bion dogmaton kai apophthegmaton ton en philosophia
> eudokimesanton, *a book that contains the only source of*
> *information available about many of the philosophers it treats*

Procrastination is the thief of time.

> —*Edward Young, 1683–1765, English poet, satirist, and*
> *rector of Welwyn. In* Night—Thoughts on Life, Death,
> and Immortality, *Young wrote a series of nine poems*
> *that gave rise to a school of "graveyard poets."*

Many businessmen—myself very much included—frequently complain that there aren't enough hours in a day to take care of the work at hand. It's true enough. The active business-man seldom has all the time to do everything that should or could be done in his business. However, no matter how busy and successful he may be, he should make time to spend with his wife and family. This not only helps to insure the success of his marriage and enables him to understand and guide his children, it adds depth and dimension to his own nature and personality.

—J. Paul Getty, 1892–1976, CEO, Getty Oil Company, from As I See It. *Jean Paul Getty became one of the first billionaires in the world. He was also married and divorced five times.*

Time has no meaning in itself unless we choose to give it significance.

> —*Leo F. Buscaglia, 1924–1998, American educator, author, and lecturer. Buscaglia believed the most important thing in life was to love, and he wrote exclusively about it. Although he never married or fathered children of his own, Buscaglia was known variously as "Dr. Hug," "the Love Merchant," and "Hug Doctor."*

It's necessary to be slightly underemployed if you are to do something significant.

> —*James Watson, b. 1928, American geneticist. Watson helped discover the molecular structure of DNA. He was awarded a Nobel Prize in 1962.*

Be focused; set boundaries on business time and personal time so you can enjoy each to the fullest. Nobody at the management level works a nine-to-five job, so it's not about that. Since technology enables us to stay plugged in as much as we'd like to, it's useful to set some boundaries on what hours and what time you want to dedicate to your job. It's really about picking the times that you can be most focused and most productive.

> —*Caroline Dorsa, b. 1959, vice president and treasurer, Merck & Company Inc.*

—TOLERANCE—

Human diversity makes tolerance more than a virtue; it makes it a requirement for survival.

> —*René Dubos, 1901–1982, French-born American bacteriologist, writer, and professor at the Rockefeller Institute, Harvard, and the State University of New York. Dubos discovered tyrocidine and gramicidin, which proved effective against pneumococcus. He also invented a method for culturing tubercle bacilli. Dubos is the author of* The Bacterial Cell.

—TRAINING—

No speech of admonition can be so fine that it will at once make those who hear it good men if they are not good already; it would surely not make archers good if they had not had previous practice in shooting; neither could it make lancers good, not horsemen; it cannot even make men able to endure bodily labor, unless they have been trained to do it before.

> —*Cyrus the Younger, 424–401 B.C., Persian prince and satrap of Asia Minor. Cyrus the Younger led an army of Asiatics and Greek mercenaries against Axtaxerxes at Cunaxa, where he was defeated and killed. This battle resulted in the famous retreat of ten thousand Greeks under Xenophon.*

When I teach my Way, I first teach by training in techniques which are easy for the pupil to understand, a doctrine which is easy to understand. I gradually endeavor to explain the deep principle, points which it is hardly possible to comprehend, according to the pupil's progress.

> —*Miyamoto Musashi, 1584–1645, Japanese Samurai ronin, from* A Book of Five Rings. *Musashi was known as "Master of the Sword."*

Neither gallantry nor heroism will avail much without professional training.

> —*Edward Cardwell, 1813–1886, British statesman. Viscount Cardwell abolished flogging as a peacetime punishment of military men. He also laid the foundations for the federation of Canada.*

Teach, teach, and teach. In my view, the most valuable manifestation of leadership behavior is when a leader continuously takes the initiative to unselfishly convey knowledge to those in his or her sphere of influence; facilitates their internalization of such knowledge; and creates a passionate environment for continuous improvement where the application of such knowledge is approached with a revolutionary spirit.

> —*Louis Laguardia, b.1948, Cuban-born American business executive and president and CEO of Human Capital Solutions Inc. Laguardia is a highly regarded authority in applied human resources management and is known for his positive, cheerful demeanor.*

—TRUST—

A man who never trusts himself never trusts anyone.

*—Paul de Gondi, 1613–1679, French statesman, cardinal de Retz,
and archbishop of Paris. Gondi led a riotous life in his youth.
He resigned as archbishop of Paris in return for rich benefices.*

No matter what may be the ability of the officer, if he loses the
confidence of his troops, disaster must sooner or later ensue.

*—Robert E. Lee, 1807–1870, American Confederate general
and military tactician and strategist. Lee commanded the
Confederate Army of Northern Virginia during the Civil War.
If ever a gentleman led an army, Lee was that gentleman.*

The man who trusts men will make fewer mistakes than he
who distrusts them.

*—Camillo Benso, 1810–1861, Italian noble, soldier, publisher,
prime minister, and conte di Cavour. Benso founded the
newspaper* Il Risorgimento. *As prime minister, he began
negotiations with Pope Pius IX for the end of temporal power of
the papacy and the establishment of Rome as Italy's capital.*

Whoever is careless with the truth in small matters cannot
be trusted with important matters.

*—Albert Einstein, 1879–1955, German-born Swiss-American
physicist. Einstein founded the theory of relativity. He was
awarded a Nobel Prize in 1921 and was a member of the
Institute for Advanced Study at Princeton University.*

The first thing a young officer must do when he joins the Army is to fight a battle, and that battle is for the hearts of his men. If he wins that battle and subsequent similar ones, his men will follow him anywhere; if he loses it, he will never do any real good.

—*Bernard Law Montgomery, 1887–1976, British field marshal and first Viscount Montgomery of Alamein. During World War II, Montgomery commanded the Allied forces in the invasion of Normandy and accepted the German surrender on May 7, 1945.*

Where large sums of money are concerned, it is advisable to trust nobody.

> —*Agatha Christie, 1890–1976, English writer who created the*
> *detectives Miss Marple and Hercule Poirot and authored*
> *the classic mystery* Murder on the Orient Express

If people can't trust you, they won't follow you. It's as simple as that. Successful leaders are individuals of strong ethical standard, people who know what they stand for, people of integrity. They set a moral compass, a sense of ethical direction, in all they undertake.

> —*Norman R. Augustine, b. 1935, American author,*
> *chairman of Lockheed Martin Corporation, assistant*
> *secretary of the army, and professor at Princeton University*

The language of truth is unadorned and always simple.

> —*Ammianus Marcellinus, c. 330–395, Roman noble,*
> *soldier, and historian. Ammianus served under*
> *Constantius II in Gaul and Persia. He is the author*
> *of* Rerum gestarum libri, *the Latin history of the*
> *Roman Empire from Nerva to the death of Valens.*

Truth is the highest thing that man may keep.

> —*Geoffrey Chaucer, c. 1340–1400, English poet*
> *and author of* The Canterbury Tales, *one of*
> *the great classics of English literature*

The general rule is, that *truth* should never be violated, because it is of the utmost importance to the comfort of life, that we should have a full security by mutual faith; and occasional inconvenience should be suffered that we may preserve it. There must, however, be some exceptions.

—*Samuel Johnson, 1709–1784, English lexicographer, essayist, and poet. Known as "Dr. Johnson," Samuel Johnson was a leading literary figure in England in his day. He is the author of* Dictionary of the English Language.

When I tell the *truth* it is not for the sake of convincing those who do not know it, but for the sake of defending those who do.

—*William Blake, 1757–1827, English artist and poet. Blake's poems mark the beginning of romanticism and the rejection of the Age of Enlightenment. He is known for his collection of poems, published as* Songs of Innocence.

Everyone wishes to have truth on his side, but it is not everyone that sincerely wishes to be on the side of truth.

—*Richard Whately, 1787–1863, English logician, author, archbishop of Dublin, and professor at Oxford. Whately satirized skepticism by reducing to absurdity the application of logic to the Scriptures in* Historic Doubts Relative to Napoleon Bonaparte.

False facts are highly injurious to the progress of science, for they endure long; but false views, if supported by some evidence, do little harm, for everyone takes a salutary pleasure in proving their falseness; and when this is done,

one path towards error is closed and the road to truth is often at the same time opened.

> —*Charles R. Darwin, 1809–1882, English natural historian and writer who advanced the theory of evolution by natural selection. His book* On the Origin of Species by Means of Natural Selection *aroused a storm of controversy that continues between evolutionists and creationists today.*

The truth is sometimes a poor competitor in the market place of ideas—complicated, unsatisfying, full of dilemmas, always vulnerable to misinterpretation and abuse.

> —*George F. Kennan, b. 1904, American author and ambassador to the Soviet Union and Yugoslavia. In 1952, Kennan became* persona non grata *in the Soviet Union after making unflattering comments about Stalin. As an author, Kennan is best known for* Russia Leaves the War. *He received Pulitzer Prizes in 1956 and 1967.*

In the war between falsehood and truth, falsehood wins the first battle and truth the last.

> —*Mujibur Rahman, 1920–1975, first prime minister of independent Bangladesh. Rahman is also known as "Sheikh Mujib."*

—WISDOM—

Keep the gold and keep the silver, but give us wisdom.

> —*Arabian proverb*

Wisdom is the supreme part of happiness.

> —*Sophocles, 496–406 B.C., Greek tragic playwright, general, and government official. Sophocles was treasurer of the Athenian Empire. He is ranked with Aeschylus and Euripides as one of the greatest Greek dramatists and is the author of* Oedipus Rex.

One part of knowledge consists in being ignorant of such things as are not worthy to be known.

>—*Crates, fl. 470–450 B.C., Greek dramatist. Crates is*
>*regarded as the founder of Greek comedy proper.*

The chief aim of wisdom is to enable one to bear with the stupidity of the ignorant.

>—*Sixtus I, d. c. 125, Roman religious leader, seventh*
>*bishop of Rome, and pope. Sixtus ruled during the*
>*reign of Hadrian and was canonized a saint.*

We must make up our minds to be ignorant of much, if we would know anything.

>—*John Henry Newman, 1801–1890, English churchman and*
>*theologian. Newman was the leader of the Tractarian or Oxford*
>*movement, opposed religious liberalism, and urged Anglican*
>*reaffirmation of the doctrine of apostolical succession. Newman*
>*became a Roman Catholic and was ordained a priest in Rome.*
>*He later became cardinal of St. George in Velabro.*

It is better to know some of the questions than all of the answers.

>—*James Thurber, 1894–1961, American cartoonist, writer,*
>*and managing editor of* The New Yorker. *Thurber is*
>*the author of* The Secret Life of Walter Mitty.

—WORKAHOLISM—

Variety's the very spice of life, that gives it all its flavor.

> —*William Cowper, 1731–1800, English poet
> best known for his long poem* The Task

One ought, every day at least, to hear a little song, read a good poem, see a fine picture, and, if it were possible, to speak a few reasonable words.

> —*Johann Wolfgang von Goethe, 1749–1832, German poet,
> dramatist, philosopher, and government official. Von Goethe was
> licensed to practice law, became privy councilor, and served
> reputably in several government positions. In late life, he gained a
> reputation as a sage, which caused him to be visited often by notable
> people from around the world. In addition to his literary works, von
> Goethe also wrote on botany, optics, and other scientific topics.*

What good is a home if you are never in it?

> —*George Grossmith, 1847–1912, English comedian, singer, and
> author; and Weedon Grossmith, 1854–1919, English writer; from*
> Diary of a Nobody. *George and Weedon Grossmith were brothers.
> George composed over six hundred humorous songs and sketches.*

No outside success can compensate for failure in the home.

> —*David O. McKay, 1873–1970, American religious leader
> and president of the Church of Jesus Christ of Latter-Day
> Saints. McKay taught that families should devote one
> evening each week to spend time together in such a way
> as to strengthen their relationships in the home.*

Don't forget until too late that the business of life is not business, but living.

—*B. C. Forbes, 1880–1954, Scottish-born American publisher of magazines. Bertie Charles Forbes was the founder, editor, and publisher of* Forbes *magazine.*

You wear yourself out in the pursuit of wealth or love or freedom, you do everything to gain some right, and once it is gained, you take no pleasure in it.

—*Oriana Fallaci, b. 1930, Italian journalist,*
editor, and writer. Fallaci received the St. Vincent
Award for Journalism in 1971 and 1973.

—WORKERS' RIGHTS—

It is an astounding anomaly that in America, this great land of the free, there should be two worlds for workers: one outside of the workplace, in which their rights are protected under the Constitution, and one *inside* the workplace, where they are substantially without rights. Our workers enjoy the least rights where they spend most of their productive time. In that one place where the most consequential events of their lives occur, where they will succeed or be swallowed up into oblivion—in that one place where they labor for their very existence—workers' rights are least in evidence and the most poorly protected.

—*Gerry Spence, b. 1929, American author, lecturer, television*
commentator, legal consultant, and founder of Trial Lawyer's
College and Lawyers and Advocates for Wyoming, in With
Justice for None. *Now steadfast in his commitment to*
representing people rather than corporations, Spence takes
pride in being a country lawyer. Nevertheless, he is widely
regarded as one of America's best trial lawyers. Spence has not
lost a jury trial since 1969 and has never lost a criminal case.

—WORRY—

Worry affects the circulation, the heart, the glands, the whole nervous system. I have never known a man who died from overwork, but many who died from doubt.

> —*Charles H. Mayo, 1856–1939, American surgeon. Along with his father, William (1819–1911), and brother, William J. (1861–1939), Charles Mayo helped the Sisters of Saint Francis found Saint Mary's Hospital in Rochester, Minnesota. The Mayos were the hospital's sole physician staff.*

I don't worry about crises anymore. I realize that I am living on borrowed time. Take things one step at a time—work toward solutions.

> —*James A. Lovell Jr., b. 1928, American navy captain, astronaut, and commander of Apollo 13, answering a question as to what he learned from the near-fatal Apollo 13 mission in an address to Pink Elephant's International Information Technology Service Management Conference & Exhibition, February 5, 2001, Disney World, Orlando, Florida. Lovell flew on four space flights, including Gemini 7, Gemini 12, Apollo 8, and Apollo 13.*

I think that at some point in your life you realize you don't have to worry if you do everything you're supposed to do right. Or if not right, if you do it the best you can. . . . What can worry do for you? You are already doing the best you can.

> —*Joe Namath, b. 1943, American football player, actor, and sports analyst. Known as "Broadway Joe" for his flamboyant bachelor-days lifestyle, Namath quarterbacked the University of Alabama to a national title before becoming the highest paid professional athlete in history on signing with the New York Jets. He stunned sports pundits by guaranteeing that the Jets would beat the Baltimore Colts in the 1969 Super Bowl, then led his team to improbable victory. He was elected to the National Football League Hall of Fame in 1985.*